"This is a well-written, useful book. Greg Bott lays out a clear, cohesive roadmap for creating lasting business wealth and success. It's a desktop bible which will empower any entrepreneur to build a strong, impenetrable financial legacy!"

F. Scott Montgomery, *CPA, CA, PFP, B.Comm. Retired Partner, Grant Thornton LLP.*

"As an entrepreneur involved in family-owned businesses, I found this book to be both practical and deeply strategic. It distils complex financial decisions into a clear roadmap for building lasting wealth and legacy, and genuinely shifts how you think, and what you do next."

Ali Damani, *Director of Operations, Ilyan Hospitality*

"If you worry about financial security, you will likely appreciate the practical advice from Dr. Bott's latest book on personal finance."

Tyrel Brochu, *MSc, Senate Director, University of Alberta*

"Greg Bott's follow-up to *Faster Safer Wealthier* is a must-read blueprint for entrepreneurs. His emphasis on the three essential asset classes for true stability is spot on. As a real estate and property management professional I have seen firsthand the consequences when entrepreneurs and investors focus only on one. The wisdom shared in this book is overdue and a must read for lasting, stress-free wealth as an entrepreneur."

Carla Browne, *Broker/Owner – Envision Real Estate Services*

"Bott introduces the practical principles that sophisticated institutional investors have long-adhered to – think in decades, diversify intelligently, and protect downside – in a concise framework entrepreneurs can execute to translate their passion for business into durable, multi-asset wealth that compounds across generations."

Dénes Németh, *ICD.D, Director of Stakeholder Relations*

"Greg offers a practical and insightful strategy for long-term wealth creation, aiming to establish a lasting legacy and financial security for future generations. His diversification model, utilizing three asset classes, is straightforward, clever, and easily actionable for busy entrepreneurs. Future generations will view the models presented in this book as a manifestation of their ancestors' dreams and aspirations."

Dr. Nizar Jaffer Somji, *DBA; M. Eng.; P. Eng.; ICD.D, Chancellor of the University of Alberta, CEO of Family Businesses*

"'... developing a plan with the end in mind...,' '... what gets measured gets done...' – I couldn't agree more with Greg's advice. His book provides an achievable roadmap for entrepreneurs looking to create balanced long-term wealth. I only wish I'd had it as a reference when I started my business 38 years ago. I also appreciate the valuable anecdotes from highly successful entrepreneurs."

Gord Gilroy, *BComm, Board Director, Founder of Vision Creative*

"This is an exceptionally well-written and highly impactful book. Dr. Greg Bott clearly articulates powerful financial principles and backs them up with practical, easy-to-follow steps for building a strong and well-balanced financial portfolio. While written from the perspective of an ambitious entrepreneur, the strategies in this book are universally applicable and can help anyone take control of their finances and build lasting wealth. Dr. Bott challenges readers to take decisive action – spend less than you earn and put your money to work – providing a clear roadmap for achieving and sustaining financial success."

Dr. Scott Wyzykoski, *DDS, BSc, Business Owner*

"After years of working closely with entrepreneurs, I've seen that many treat their business as their main retirement plan. While this has worked for some, Greg's book delivers a thorough guide to help all entrepreneurs build a more secure retirement. Greg explains that your business should be just one part of a well-rounded strategy, complemented by a sound investment plan incorporating investing in market indexes, and residential real estate. I recommended Greg's new book for entrepreneurs and their families seeking practical, real-world advice for long-term financial well-being."

George Coon, *FCPA, FCMA, ICD.D, CFP,*
Retired Corporate Banker

"If you're looking to build a life of purpose and fulfilment through a deliberate strategy, this book is for you. It provides a high-level overview of the key metrics that matter in both business and life, while shining a light on what far too many entrepreneurs miss when they become consumed by the daily grind."

Arshad Rashed, *Brokerage Owner and Real Estate*
Entrepreneur, Century 21 Bravo Realty

"I thoroughly enjoyed Greg's book and recommend it to those looking to plan for long term financial security and personal freedom. My personal journey is closely aligned with Greg's advice about saving, investing and diversification. He is right that these attributes combined with entrepreneurship, patience and a long-term vision will provide you and your family with meaningful security."

Dave Rumbold, *P.Eng, FEC, Board Director*

"Dr. Gregory Bott's *Rethink Your Financial Purpose* offers entrepreneurs a smart, practical approach to building wealth that endures beyond the business itself. Grounded in real-world experience, the book outlines a practical framework built on three core asset classes – business ownership, index funds, and real estate – showing how they work together to create stability, independence, and long-term wealth. Dr. Bott's advice is approachable, actionable, and relevant whether you are early in your journey or refining an established financial plan. More than a wealth-building manual, this book challenges entrepreneurs to think intentionally about legacy, purpose, and the impact they leave behind. A valuable read for any business owner ready to plan with confidence and build a future that endures."

Diana Ly, *MBA, Founding Partner, p's & q's Consulting, Director at the Alberta Advanced Manufacturing International Hub, University of Alberta*

Rethink Your Financial Purpose

As a seminal writing on personal finances for business owners, this book details a step-by-step guide to how an entrepreneur can use their business as a springboard for acquiring and protecting exponential wealth.

You've heard the stories of successful businesses failing and their founders undergoing personal financial hardship. This practical guide reveals how to build wealth that remains intact, even when your company faces challenges. Every business owner undergoes significant periods of stress during inevitable business downturns or even changes to personal circumstances. While most entrepreneurs pour everything into their businesses, the wisest build a financial resilience that can withstand inevitable downturns.This book shows you exactly how to do it through presenting a proven three-asset-class framework and step-by-step methods to acquire and maintain wealth during any economic condition. It outlines common financial pitfalls that derail even the most successful business owners and presents a decision-making framework for evaluating new financial opportunities as well as the small, consistent actions that combine into longer-term growth. In this book, you'll discover:

- How to really understand your definition of success;
- The dashboard you will reference regularly to keep you on course;

- The step-by-step strategy to acquire impenetrable assets;
- The stumbling blocks that trip up the unprepared entrepreneur;
- How to process new information and understand if it fits in your plan;
- How seemingly small decisions have big long-term payoffs.

This book is essential reading for business owners and entrepreneurs who want to protect their personal finances from business fluctuations, seek to build intergenerational wealth beyond their primary business and need practical strategies to navigate financial stress during downturns.

Gregory Bott is an entrepreneur, investor, university instructor, board director and thought leader. As a governance and leadership expert with four degrees across three continents, he has become a sought-after board director, currently serving on boards in the areas of post-secondary education, social services and agricultural commodities. He was recently awarded Top 40 Under 40 for community leadership. As an entrepreneur, he has owned and operated numerous businesses across multiple industries, including hospitality, real estate and agriculture. Author of the best-selling book, *Faster Safer Wealthier: Skip the Start-up and Buy a Stable Business to Build Intergenerational Wealth*, he is an expert in the areas of business acquisitions, wealth accumulation and in becoming your best future self.

GREGORY BOTT

Rethink Your Financial Purpose

Every Entrepreneur's Guide to Guaranteed Family Wealth Accumulation and Retention

Routledge
Taylor & Francis Group
LONDON AND NEW YORK

First published 2027
by Routledge
4 Park Square, Milton Park, Abingdon, Oxon OX14 4RN

and by Routledge
605 Third Avenue, New York, NY 10158

Routledge is an imprint of the Taylor & Francis Group, an informa business

British Library Cataloguing-in-Publication Data
A catalogue record for this book is available from the British Library

ISBN: 978-1-041-20794-8 (hbk)
ISBN: 978-1-041-16838-6 (pbk)
ISBN: 978-1-003-72424-7 (ebk)

DOI: 10.4324/9781003724247

Typeset in Joanna MT
by Newgen Publishing UK

Contents

To Achieve More You Must Become More

One

If circumstances were to cause your business to flounder or, worse, fail, would your personal finances still be in great shape, and would you still be able to achieve the legacy you desire to leave? If you answered "no", then you need this book.

Jennifer Needed This Book

As a young girl, everyone told Jennifer that she had potential and was going to be very successful one day. She graduated from university and continued to hear this compliment repeated by classmates, family and friends. In her late twenties, she started her first business, which was a success. She was on top of the world with a staff of 40 before the age of 30.

She focused all her efforts, occasionally taking stock of the business and was on course to be a millionaire by the age of 35. But as time went on, the business landscape in her industry became more competitive and sales dropped. She was still making money, but her income drastically declined.

She then found herself approaching 40 with fewer employees and a fraction of the net worth she had projected just a few years back. Her once million-dollar business was now worth a fraction of what it was. But what hit harder was that the lady looking back at her in the mirror had not lived up to the potential of years past.

DOI: 10.4324/9781003724247-1

Once on top of the world, she now felt like a failure. Stressed about money, her anxiety became a daily drain. Tasks once performed with ease seemed to drag on, as she had lost energy.

Her friends still saw her as they always had – successful, talented and leading a purposeful life. They still looked up to her and sought out her advice. Yet she felt like a failure. She had put her whole life into one bucket and placed the full weight of her success on her business. The success of her business, and thus her net worth, had become so intertwined with her self-worth. When one fell, the other fell even harder.

Since her business had been a success, she had not felt the need to consider her personal finances along the way. Why would she need to bother with minuscule details of low returns offered in a pension plan when her business had been a success? Why would she reroute funds towards an index fund when she could keep it in her business and reinvest in the equipment that she required to grow the business? Afterall, she could compound wealth at an exponential rate compared to what her friends were receiving in the stock market.

This caused her to reflect deeply and ask: "How come this girl, who everyone loved, who had so much potential, who worked so hard, had not reached her potential?"

The truth is, there is a little bit of Jennifer in every entrepreneur.

The reality is that many entrepreneurs tend to focus their full net worth on their business. Financially, physically and mentally. We are so focused that our net worth becomes synonymous with our personal worth.

When you are all in on your business, when it hits a low – and it will hit a low – you will be both financially and emotionally devastated. Your mental health will take a toll.

Without a more holistic approach to finances, our net worth is subject to the cyclicality that haunts every business.

Without a structural financial intervention, most entrepreneurs, just like Jennifer, continue to witness turbulent fluctuations and sharp declines to both their wealth and mental health, over and over, for the remainder of their lives. It is stressful. It isn't what you thought you signed up for when you started your company.

The good news is that Jennifer was able to pick herself up, executing the philosophies outlined in this book. The financial system that she now follows has created an impenetrable moat around her financial worth. She is happy, fulfilled and she has created impenetrable intergenerational wealth! Oh, and her heirs will be rich!

How did she do it? Read on to find out.

Your Future Self

Your future financial independence should not be dependent on the whims of endless forces out of your control pressing upon a singular asset – your business.

Following the approach in this book, your business will simply be one asset within your impenetrable *entrepreneurial financial strategic plan*. When it experiences a temporary dip, you won't have to panic because your overarching portfolio is purposeful, vast and resilient.

Your future financial self will remain unfazed by the loss of your largest client, the death of a business partner, a closure resulting from a pandemic, or the inability to sell your business in a downturn upon retirement.

Your business should be a bonus to your retirement and your estate, not the whole basket. If you cash out in the millions in your business exit, that is great, but what if that does not occur as planned? It won't matter, as it is just one portion within a greater strategy.

What This Book is About

There are three asset classes required for every entrepreneur to achieve an *Impenetrable Financial Legacy* and build substantial and enduring intergenerational wealth: business ownership, index funds and real estate. I include an outline of the intricacies of each and detail how each of these vehicles works together, whether you are currently a business owner or plan to be in the future.

Building an Impenetrable Financial Legacy is easy. That is, when you define easy as something that you can do by following the tracks of those who have achieved it. If you have the mental resolve to be a business owner, you have the mental capacity to build a financial legacy.

You can build intergenerational wealth, your index funds will be diversified across all sectors and not be reliant on a single stock or single industry, your business will have a risk mitigation strategy set up to withstand severe storms and your real estate properties will produce appreciation and staying power in your portfolio. You will own multiple asset classes that are uncorrelated – when one is down, the other can continue to build your future.

For you, there is a fortress protecting your empire that others do not have.

Planned out this way gives you options. If you want to hand down your properties or business to the next generation, you can live off your stock portfolio; if one asset class is down at the time of retirement, sell a different one; if one is highly taxed, you have others that do not count as income upon drawing down on them.

I will demonstrate how simple it is to build a multimillion-dollar personal net worth using your business as a springboard and how such asset classes complement each other. It is simply a matter of following a purposeful plan and then practising good financial habits, month after month, year after year.

Your wealth to date is an accumulation of the person you have become, of the decisions you have made up to now. Your wealth will only grow to the extent that you are willing to grow. Reading this book is but one minor step – you must read hundreds of books, associate with those of who you admire, seek feedback, set goals and be a sponge for knowledge.

The first lesson: Sophisticated entrepreneurs, concerned with their financial legacy, think long term.

You should view your holdings as a family office – an entity that will continue throughout generations – and your retirement is not a trigger to change course as it would be for others. The wealthy think in 100-year cycles, not in life stages.

You will be delighted to hear throughout the book how Jennifer has been enlightened to a new philosophy, which has been the catalyst for restructuring her financial paradigm. She has moved from feeling defeated, stressed and near broke, to being on a path towards guaranteed intergenerational wealth. She is building an Impenetrable Financial Legacy.

As an entrepreneur with an Impenetrable Financial Legacy, with assets across index funds, real estate and privately held businesses, she now has the luxury of continuing to grow her net worth during retirement and not to draw down on it.

She has a long-term outlook. Her future self is being served by her discipline of today.

She has further shifted her philosophy from one's net worth being their individual personal wealth, to a philosophy of family wealth, whereby she is simply the custodian of it for future generations.

She is proud of the businesses that she is creating. She plans for their valuations to keep growing, provide cash flow into her retirement and to be sold for great sums. But she is not reliant on them. They are simply one asset in her portfolio – and their values are merely a bonus to the recipients of her estate.

This book is for every business owner with an entrepreneurial spirit who wants to build a legacy beyond simply having been a business owner.

About the Author

I am just a farm boy from Alberta, with a passion for business, wealth, teaching and improving the lives of those on this journey alongside me. As with most entrepreneurs, my story has paralleled the story of Jennifer – a quick energy and success out of the gate, then seemingly catastrophic failures, providing for wonderful lessons.

I want you to succeed and to scale the hurdles that have a hold on every business owner. I want to share with you the knowledge base that I have accumulated from my successes and failures. From lessons learned from ownership of businesses across multiple industries, including hospitality, real estate and agriculture. And having taught business and economics to university students.

I never quit learning. My library continues to grow. My circle of friends, far smarter than myself, continues to grow. I am convinced that this is the result of seeking out those who I admire, not as a result of my shrinking intelligence. I am surrounded by people with a positive outlook, who enjoy what they do and who have a vision beyond themselves.

Where you are in life is an accumulation of who you have chosen to become. If this is true, the opposite must also be true. If you are unhappy with your present situation and you want things to change, you must change.

If you plan your journey very purposefully, you will arrive at a very desirable destination – one with financial freedom, having a breadth and depth of relationships and doing the things you enjoy with the people you love. A purposeful plan with the resolve of discipline will further provide for the best chances of longevity of positive physical and mental health.

The philosophies in this book are based on my experiences in business, education, research and university teaching.

My wish is that readers grasp a better understanding of the landmines of traditional thinking in entrepreneurship that cause inevitable financial hardship. It doesn't have to be that way.

I wish for you to think bigger, think deeper and to develop an intentional plan for a very purposeful life. To do this, you must think more holistically about your financial legacy.

Achieving an Intentional Life

Two

RELATIONSHIPS, HEALTH AND EXPONENTIAL WEALTH

How do you define success? Envision your ideal future self – how do you feel, where are you, who are you with, what aspects of your life do you no longer worry about and what areas of your life are you most proud of?

For many, success can be defined as "the ability to live your life the way you want to live it, doing what you most enjoy, surrounded by people you admire and respect" (Tracy, 2017, p. xv).

Brian Tracy (2017), author of over 70 books and an authority on human potential and personal effectiveness, suggests that all humans have four goals in common: being healthy and fit, having excellent relationships, being able to do what we love, and achieving financial independence. I would argue that these are not mutually exclusive and having success in one area has an influence on the successes in other areas of your life.

"Everything involves relationships. Virtually all of your problems in life will come as a result of your entering into wrong relationships with the wrong people. Virtually all of your great successes in life will be accompanied by great relationships with good people who help you and whom you help in return" (Tracy, 2001, p. 58).

DOI: 10.4324/9781003724247-2

Warren Buffett defines success as being loved by those you wish to have love you.

The happiest retirees who I know never retire. They may not work in a traditional sense, but they continue to find purpose in the community. They stay healthy and happy by having a purpose and staying active. They volunteer, operate companies, manage their portfolios, consult and continue to make significant decisions.

My friend Gloria is a great example of this. She and her husband travel extensively, recently doing treks that would make someone my age nervous. In her mid 80s, she is on multiple boards, shows up at community events to support friends and colleagues and always picks up the phone when someone requires some wisdom, me included.

While health, relationships and freedom to do what we want are equally important, this book focuses on financial independence. But each of these pillars cannot be considered in isolation. Jim Rohn (1930-2009) says it best:

> All disciplines affect each other. In fact, here is a good philosophical phrase: Everything affects everything else. Nothing stands alone. Don't be naïve in saying well this doesn't matter. I am telling you that everything matters. There are some things that matter more than others. But there isn't anything that doesn't matter. We all pity the man who says, well this is the only place that I let down. Not true. Key to take home. Every let down affects the rest of your performance. ... If you don't take the walk around the block, you probably won't do the apple a day. If you don't do the apple a day, you probably won't start building your library. If you don't build your library, you probably won't keep a journal, you won't take pictures, you won't do this ...

you won't do wise things with your money. You won't do wise things with your time. You won't do wise things with your possibilities and your relationships. The first thing that you know, six years of that has accumulated and we say, you have messed up. The whole key to reversing this process now is to start picking up these disciplines. Now here is the positive side: every new discipline affects the rest of your disciplines. Every new one affects the rest. That is why action is so important. The least action. The smallest action. Take it. Because when you start accomplishing and the value starts to return from that one action, it will inspire you to do the next one and the next one and the next one. You start walking around the block, it will inspire you to get an apple, you get an apple, it will inspire you to get a book, you get a book it will inspire you to get a journal, you get a journal it will inspire you to grow, develop some skills. All disciplines affect each other. Every lack affects the rest. Every new affects the rest... the key is to diminish the lack and set up the new. And you started a whole new life process.

(Rohn, J. *Don't live a small life* podcast, 1 June, 2021)

In this book, I will show you how to build an Impenetrable Financial Legacy, ultimately leading to financial independence and freedom not only for you, but for your heirs. You must seek knowledge and discipline in the other areas of your life – e.g. health and relationships – in order to live a complete life.

As Stanley and Danko (2010, p. 46) say "[f]inancially independent people are happier than those in their same income/age cohort who are not financially secure". That sounds pretty cool. Let's aim for that!

The most basic definition of financial independence is when you have built a net worth whereby the earnings from your assets provide for your living expenses for the remainder of your life. However, this book doesn't stop there. We take your wealth further.

In this book, I will demonstrate how you can become financially complete. I will show you how to become a multi-millionaire, ultimately building an Impenetrable Financial Legacy – intergenerational wealth within a fortress, whereby you can continue to live off the returns, well into retirement, while your net worth continues to grow.

Only you can choose by what age you want to be financially independent, and what sacrifices you are willing to make to get there. You may plan to work into your retirement age, but I strongly suggest that you plan to be financially independent well before then – perhaps before the age of 60 – so that continuing to work is an *option*, not a *necessity*. Even if we wish to continue to work, our health is never guaranteed and that becomes more pronounced with age.

Having a focus on your mental and physical health provides the energy required for focusing on your business. Achieving financial independence is paramount to your mental health – not having to worry about when you will be able to retire, or not being self-sufficient if your health suffers. All areas of your life are connected.

Achieving financial independence is not hard, nor is it complicated.

Why then do the vast majority of business owners incur catastrophic setbacks, large swings in their net worth and periods of intense stress and poor mental health? Because they are so distracted with their business that they have not been intentional about planning their life. And often ignore financial flows beyond the workings of their daily business grind.

And why then are most of the greater population not only not financially independent, but are so far away from it that they are living paycheque to paycheque? Because it is also easy to not do the steps required to become financially independent. The lure of consumerism – spending today out of envy for consumer items possessed by those around them – prioritizes immediate gratification of wants and desires in the present over the needs of our future selves and the needs of our children and heirs.

Entrepreneurs also fall on the extremes of the spectrum; on one extreme, their business is their whole net worth. On the other extreme, they overcomplicate their finances by jumping on every new idea that comes to mind. But extremes are dangerous, and an inevitable formula for disaster – financial disaster, eventually affecting your relationships and mental health.

I will demonstrate the three asset classes – and only three – required for an entrepreneur to build enduring wealth: business ownership, index funds and real estate. This book includes an outline of the intricacies of each, as well as how each of these asset classes work together.

Why Three Asset Classes?

Proper asset allocation is not only important for risk mitigation but also for mental health. Having all your eggs in one basket – your business – means that when your business is going well, so are your personal finances. But when your business struggles, so do your personal finances. Having the two as the same provides for significant swings in the health of your finances, as well as your mental health.

A more focused intentionality of asset allocation provides you with options. If you want to hand your properties or business to the next generation, you can live off your stock portfolio; if one asset class is down at the time of retirement, sell a different one; if one is highly taxed, you have others that do not count as income upon accessing them.

IT'S POSSIBLE EVERYTHING YOU'VE LEARNED ABOUT FINANCES IS WRONG

Just like Jennifer, in my early tenure with entrepreneurship, I had been exposed to a different set of teachings and philosophies than what I can now present in this book.

And I can list many others that I admire who have had major setbacks in business. One business owner and good friend went from aggressive expansion and personal chauffeurs to significant business retraction and closures of numerous stores that they had expanded into. While a significant number of others have been the victim of the unexpected.

Life events such as divorce, deteriorating health of themselves or of a family member are common occurrences; real estate or stock market crashes; high inflation; increased interest rates and economic cycles can wreak havoc on any business.

Their mistakes are usually only obvious in retrospect. The temporary adrenaline of success can be the enemy of endurance.

Like Jennifer, I felt that because I could compound wealth at a better rate within businesses that I invested in and operated, I could ignore other asset classes. My accountants and advisers seemed to agree with this.

I went many years thinking that I was ahead of my peers because my net worth, on paper, was well ahead of my benchmarked peer group. But despite the best laid plans, no business is without risk. If your business valuation drops, you will be left with both your business and your personal net worth not being in order.

As someone who finds success in entrepreneurial endeavours, it is very likely that your business will become your largest asset class. This is almost inevitable, not because your other asset classes are insignificant, but because with success, this asset in particular is expected to grow exponentially. It is therefore quite easy to disregard the importance of such other asset classes – your personal finances – and of obtaining multiple streams of current and future income.

There are many reasons to hold multiple asset classes:

- Diversification in holdings stabilizes your wealth;
- It allows for multiple streams of income;
- Holding uncorrelated assets allows for increased net worth across most economic environments;
- Each asset class holds different characteristics – taxable/non-taxable, appreciation/cash flow, growth/stable;
- There are learnings and synergies that come from holding each asset class that can be applied to the others; and,
- It forces you to change your thinking from business owner to the custodian of significant intergenerational wealth for future generations.

By considering yourself the chief executive officer and chief investment officer of your family office, you can separate the two. In such a case, if your business has a bad quarter or year, it has no immediate impact on your personal finances. Your retirement plan does not need to be sacrificed. Your real estate assets, your index funds and other investments continue to produce as they should.

How do you define success? How would financial independence change your life, your happiness, your mental and physical health, your ability to do the things that you love? Make a simple choice to achieve it, for you, your family, and your heirs.

Who are the wealthy and what can we learn from them? This will be explored in the next chapter.

REFERENCES

Rohn, Jim. *Jim Rohn Talks*, podcast. "Don't Live a Small Life." June 1, 2021.

Stanley, Thomas J., and William D. Danko. *The Millionaire Next Door: The Surprising Secrets of America's Wealthy*. Taylor Trade Publishing, 2010.

Tracy, Brian. *The 21 Secrets of Self-Made Millionaires: How to Achieve Independence Faster and Easier Than You Ever Thought Possible*. Executive Books, 2001.

Tracy, Brian. *Million Dollar Habits: Proven Power Practices to Double & Triple Your Income*. Entrepreneur Press, 2017.

Three

PROTOTYPING THE WEALTHY

Many people make a significant income but fail to ever become wealthy. They simply spend what they earn. And often more than they earn. Whether this occurs slowly or rapidly, it is financial suicide.

Stanley and Danko (2010, p. 1) similarly note, "Wealth is not the same as income. If you make a good income each year and spend it all, you are not getting wealthier. You are just living high. Wealth is what you accumulate, not what you spend".

Becoming wealthy is simple. It isn't easy, but it is simple. Simply study what it is that the affluent do differently than the general population, and then do that. Follow the steps laid out in this book to build and protect your wealth.

Who are the affluent and what do they do differently? The attributes of a millionaire are detailed in the 2010 book by Stanley and Danko who spent their careers interviewing and surveying millionaires. The authors found that the typical millionaire is self-employed, a homeowner, first generation affluent, with very few having ever received an inheritance, live well below their means, do not drive new cars, are fastidious investors – investing nearly 20% of their household income each year – and hold about 20% of their household's

DOI: 10.4324/9781003724247-3

wealth in the stock market, rarely selling such investments. Each of these points are addressed in this book.

One study similarly found that nearly nine out of ten millionaires in America have made their own wealth: "[T]hey started with nothing, and in many cases came from extreme poverty" (Cumberland, 2019, p. 20). An individual's economic starting point is therefore irrelevant to where they end up on the financial spectrum. This suggests that no matter where you start, you can become financially independent.

The untrained eye can easily be fooled into believing people with fancy cars, big houses and lavish holidays are wealthy. The opposite is more likely to be true. Most millionaires are "hiding in plain sight" (Hogan, 2019). Like my buddy Jesse, who drives a truck that is about 30 years old, does his own oil changes and washes his vehicle at home, or my friend Parag, who rarely dines out, or my colleague who adds extra water to canned soup, or our family friends who cut out all streaming services.

Wealth is more likely to be the daily discipline, contentment with what you have, the unspent luxuries, the rusty vehicles and the unpretentious, unassuming demeanour.

Personal finance author Chris Hogan (2019, p. 7) says it best: "Listen, there is absolutely no reason why someone with the right information shouldn't retire with at least $1 million in net worth. It doesn't matter where you live or what you do. It doesn't matter what your parents have or don't have. It doesn't matter if you'll get an inheritance or not. Those are all excuses broke people use to explain why they aren't winning. Your wealth-building potential comes down to one – and only one – person, and that's you".

It has been suggested that if all the money in the world were to be taken away and then distributed equally among the population, it would soon end up back in the same hands. And I firmly believe this to be true because the journey to wealth is not about the amount of money that you have, but about who you become in the process. Those who follow a disciplined approach and do things that the wealthy do accumulate wealth.

Anyone can become wealthy. It is simply a choice to undertake certain behaviours consistently over time. Study what they do and do that. It's not easy, but it is simple.

As a business owner, you have a running head start. You already have a cash-flowing asset that acts as the catalyst to wealth accumulation. Your business can serve as the pillar of wealth accumulation if you, first, set it up to be around for the long term and, second, you build a financial moat, as you will learn in this book.

A STEP-BY-STEP GUIDE TO DR BOTT'S IMPENETRABLE FINANCIAL LEGACY

When Jennifer's business was struggling, she finally realized that it was time to see what impact the drop in sales was having on her personal net worth, so she completed a net worth statement.

Once proud of what she had achieved, being within reach of being a millionaire while at a young age, her current economic status was a mere fraction of what it once was.

Now her balance sheet told her that she was only worth $300,000. Her business made up about $200,000 after subtracting her equipment loan. Jennifer had $45,000 equity in her house after accounting for her mortgage, a vehicle worth $25,000, but a loan of $15,000. She also had cash in savings of $20,000, $5,000 in credit card debt and $30,000 in various stocks. She had sold the rest of her stocks to invest in her business.

After running a business for a number of years, this is not a picture of wealth. Throughout this book, we will compare her decision making to that of someone who is building sustainable intergenerational wealth, someone who is building an Impenetrable Financial Legacy.

Once she realized the impact that her business slowdown was having on her net worth, Jennifer was emotionally paralyzed. She felt defeated. It took a toll on her mental health and on her relationships. How could she have worked so hard with so little payoff? What had she done wrong to end up at age 35 with a regression in her financial state?

Jennifer had not set up her business for success. Following the steps in the chapter on stable business ownership will ensure that your business remains profitable and endures for the long run.

She had placed all her efforts, all her net worth, into her business. In this book, you will learn how to set up your personal finances so that you barely feel the effects of a business downturn.

Take Stock of Your Personal Balance Sheet

The wealthy know where they stand financially – always and continuously. They know how much they are worth today and how much they will be worth next year.

The affluent know where each dollar goes *before* they ever receive it. They do not look back upon a year gone by and say, "Oops, where did it all go?" They have a meticulous understanding of their inflows and outflows and of how each dollar is to be allocated among consumables, daily living, education and investments.

What you measure grows. What you focus on grows. If it is wealth that you seek, you must take very deliberate steps to track and grow your wealth. You must be extremely cognizant of how money flows in and out of your life, how your personal financial decisions affect your business and how your business affects your personal life.

While tracking your income and expenses is important to know that your investment goals are on track, it is more important to focus on your balance sheet than to remain fixated on increased earnings.

In fact, in a study of 10,000 millionaires, Hogan found that 69% of millionaires had not averaged $100,000 in household income, and 31% had never had a six-figure income in any single working year. Millionaire status is thus not about big paycheques; it is a mindset, a discipline.

Only once you can tangibly and accurately see where you are at can you make educated adjustments to your asset mix. The first step in wealth accumulation is to understand your current financial status, develop a plan with the end in mind and track it frequently.

I suggest quarterly to keep it at the top of your mind. When choosing a shorter time frame, you may become not only obsessed with it, but also become fixated on short-term fluctuations. Intervals that are too infrequent do not provide the proper facilitation to make the required adjustments to your money flow patterns.

Not until you take stock and see it written down can you see where your wealth is held. Start by creating a personal net worth statement. Write down all your assets and liabilities.

Assets – What You Own

Assets might include real estate, publicly traded stocks, your business, pension plans, cash value of life insurance and bank account balances.

If you can come up with a range for an asset valuation, record the more conservative estimate. Be honest with yourself and do not overvalue any particular asset.

Most business owners do not have an accurate estimation of the value of their business. I suggest speaking with those who have a strong ability to value companies, or with colleagues who have bought and sold businesses. Again, take steps to not overestimate the value.

If you are a consultant without staff or have a business with gross revenue under $500,000, it is best to put zero for the value of the business, as the value of a third-party sale of your business is uncertain. There is a chance that, until you can grow the company, it will not have any significant exit valuation. I am not suggesting that the business has no value to your journey, but simply that the resale value is uncertain.

Once you have a complete list of your assets, organize them into categories so that you can get a clear picture of your asset allocation – how much of your net worth is tied up in your business, in your real estate and in the stock market.

Liabilities – What You Owe

Next, write down all your liabilities. Liabilities will typically include mortgages, business loans, lines of credit, student debt, credit card balances and other loans.

Once you have this starting point, you can see any risks and vulnerabilities that you have.

Here is what a typical balance sheet might look like after just a few years of following my Impenetrable Financial Legacy method:

Personal daily finances

Personal cash in bank accounts
Cash in education account (or other savings categories that are important to achieving your personal plan)
Personal home
Personal line of credit
Credit card balance

Net value of personal finances

Index funds and life insurance

TFSA
RRSP
Non-tax advantaged accounts
Cash value of life insurance

Total value of investments

Real estate

Property one
Property two
Property three

Mortgage on property one
Mortgage on property two
Mortgage on property three

Net value of residential real estate positions

Business ownership

Gross value of business one
Business debt
Net value of business one

Gross value of business two

Business debt
Net value of business two

Assets minus liabilities = your net worth.

Updating your net worth statement quarterly will help you to identify trends and will ensure you remain focused on wealth accumulation.

Some observations that you might observe from tracking your net worth include:

- Holding onto assets that are underproducing. Selling them would provide cash to invest into a better return;
- Identifying an overallocation in one area of your portfolio and an underallocation in other areas. Reallocating would reduce your exposure to certain risks;
- The ability to seek feedback from trusted advisers, who will be able to make recommendations to improving your plan and help to de-risk any vulnerabilities. Advisers can be paid advisers or people who are ahead of you financially;
- Identifying risk areas, such as high debt levels, creating a vulnerability to increases in interest rates;
- Asset and account balances will be readily available to provide to lenders when you require debt for that next business or property;
- When benchmarked against a plan, you will see if you are on track with your goals for each category as well as overall and are then able to adjust accordingly.

Having a written plan also provides for motivation and accountability. You will be able to observe the trends in your wealth. For example, I did not have an appreciation for the real estate that I was holding until I properly tracked the trends within my holdings. I could then see how much mortgage was being paid down each year and had a better understanding of the gross value and equity held within the portfolio.

Seeing my real estate tracked in this way also exposed some vulnerabilities I had in cash flow if interest rates were to increase. I had previously included real estate in my personal balance sheet as net equity. However, after seeing it with gross property values and total debt separated, I was able identify that real estate held a larger allocation in my portfolio than I had intended.

I was also then able to run some scenarios on interest rate increases to see the consequences an interest rate increase would have on cash flow. Following this exercise, I sold two properties and reallocated funds to other asset classes that had been relatively neglected.

Update Your Net Worth Quarterly

Updating your net worth every three months will help you to identify trends and ensure that you remain focused on wealth accumulation.

It is important to use it as a guiding tool and not to become fixated on it. There will be years in which you may see a decrease – perhaps the stock market is down, or your business loses a major client, decreasing the valuation of your company. Recognize that there will be cyclical components within your asset listing.

A decrease does not define you. More likely than not, a down market identifies a buying opportunity. But it is important to see the trends and to determine if a negative trend is exposing a vulnerability in your plan or if it is simply the result of a cyclical trend that will soon be self-correcting. Down markets follow up markets. Up markets follow down markets.

Share your net worth statement with trusted advisers in your circle. This doesn't just mean a paid adviser, but high-net-worth individuals who you respect. Share your goals openly so that others can help to identify any opportunities and vulnerabilities in your plan. Too many people keep their finances private. By openly discusing them with those of whom you trust, you advance your knowledge.

I was lucky enough to sit next to a financial planner on a flight to Japan. Discovering this an hour before landing provided just enough time to pull my financial plan out of my bag and deep dive into my asset allocation. Thanks, random stranger!

It is important to find that sweet spot of taking serious action and instituting discipline, but stopping one inch shy of becoming obsessed with your net worth, remembering that "it doesn't tell you what you're worth as a person, only what you're worth in monetary terms" (Rohn, 1996, p. 104).

Every entrepreneur should own investments within the three asset classes, namely index funds, real estate and of course, your business ownership. But *how* you invest within each asset class is of the utmost importance.

In the following sections, I will walk you through each, including why they are important to own in addition to your business, how to choose each investment, investment levels required and how they work together, including the different tax implications and liquidity of each.

REFERENCES

Cumberland, Nigel. *100 Things Millionaires Do: Little Lessons in Creating Wealth*. Nicholas Brealey Publishing, 2019.

Hogan, Chri. *Everyday Millionaires: How Ordinary People Build Extraordinary Wealth – and How You Can Too*. Ramsey Press, 2019.

Rohn, Jim. *7 Strategies for Wealth & Happiness: Power Ideas from America's Foremost Business Philosopher*. Three Rivers Press, 1996.

Stanley, Thomas J., and William D. Danko. *The Millionaire Next Door: The Surprising Secrets of America's Wealthy*. Taylor Trade Publishing, 2010.

Asset One: Stable Business Ownership

Four

AN ENTREPRENEUR AND AN INVESTOR

The astute entrepreneur must think like both an entrepreneur and an investor.

Business ownership is the staple wealth-building asset class for entrepreneurs and arguably the single most effective method to build intergenerational wealth within a generation.

Entrepreneurs have found a way to remove the cap on potential earnings. It is therefore not surprising that Stanley and Danko, authors of *The Millionaire Next Door*, found that "self-employed people make up less than 20 percent of the workers in America but account for two-thirds of the millionaires" (2010, p. 8). Business ownership can be your conduit to achieving wealth.

When you are an employee, you are often required to be at a certain place at a certain time to receive your pay cheque. And such earnings are further dependent upon how many hours in a day you are focused on building someone else's wealth at the expense of not creating time for the areas of greatest impact to your own life. You are not in control of your most valuable resource – your time.

When your main source of income comes from business ownership – a source that is not directly correlated to your time – you can choose to allocate your time to areas of greatest

DOI: 10.4324/9781003724247-4

impact on your life, whether that be time with family, your health, nurturing relationships, self-development or investing and asset allocation, including business acquisitions.

Business ownership is the foundation of an entrepreneur's wealth, upon which personal finances and the building of other asset classes are based. It provides the entrepreneur with their salary to eat, live, travel, support their family and invest.

You are in control of the direction of your company. Every effort that you put in has the potential to provide exponential rewards. Every decision that you make has an impact on your wealth – for better or for worse. You are in the driver's seat. You determine the growth; you determine the risk-reward trade-off; you determine how much retained earnings stay in the business for future investment and growth (long-term orientation) versus how much you take as your yearly salary (short-term orientation).

But not all businesses are created equally. And not all businesses have the staying power to retain true, enduring wealth.

As an astute entrepreneur, you have to answer two foundational questions:

1) You must think like an investor. Is this the right business for building substantial and sustainable wealth?
2) How do I set up my existing and/or future business(es) to be an enduring business that contributes to such wealth in perpetuity?

The following sections walk you through these two fundamental assessments, detailing how to ensure your business adds to your wealth consistently for the long run.

Acquired vs Start-up

If you do not yet have an established cash-flowing business, you have to decide whether to start a company from scratch or to acquire an existing business.

Start-ups have a significantly higher failure rate compared to established businesses and thus tend to not provide a palatable risk-reward trade-off. With a start-up, it is more "likely that you end up getting less money than you would in a salaried position and yet, you spend more time at the office than at home. And there's the real prospect that the business you've spent money, time and energy nurturing from inception won't last more than five years" (Jay, 2019, p. 11).

If you are not yet a business owner, I strongly encourage you to consider buying an established business. "Through a truly objective lens, the financial return on investment, especially when placing a value on your time, is not conducive to a start-up. The math just doesn't add up" (Bott, 2021, p. 66).

To undertake a start-up is to take on a risk. You must ensure that there is a reason for that risk (risk = probability of reduced wealth), a reason to carry a loss for an extended period of time (lost cash = reduced wealth) and to spend time on unremunerative tasks when you could be working on high-level functions of an established company (time on small things = delayed wealth).

I have done this. And many others have. Some have succeeded and some have not. But why take on unnecessary headwinds? Have you ever placed yourself in a situation of running out of cash and not knowing where the next injection will come from to fund payroll? This isn't in alignment with peace of mind and financial freedom.

With an existing business, you are buying: a recurring revenue stream with a proven history; an existing customer base; tested and refined products or services that have proven to provide value to the customer base; a complete team, including leadership and a staff that understands the operations and can maintain customer relationships; existing systems, such as ordering, inventory, operations and accounting and; existing vendor relationships.

The proven history of an established business exponentially reduces the risk of business ownership when compared to a start-up. When the end goal is wealth, buying an established business accelerates your journey by many years.

To dive further into the benefits of buying an established business and the process of doing so (anyone can do this!), I refer you to my book titled *Faster Safer Wealthier: Skip the Start-up and Buy a Stable Business to Build Intergenerational Wealth*.

Regardless of whether you obtained your business through the start-up grind or by acquiring an existing business, the next step is to manage risk within your business so that you ensure that it adds to your wealth over the long run.

Remember: You must think like both an entrepreneur and an investor to build intergenerational wealth within a generation.

CHOOSE AN ENDURING BUSINESS

Dull Businesses and Enduring Profitability

Choose a business that has fundamentals consistent with not only wealth accumulation but, more importantly, with wealth retention.

Warren Buffett uses the term "durable competitive advantage" to refer to companies that show signs of lasting profitability. Such businesses tend to be in less cyclical industries and provide products that users require across all stages of the economic cycle.

There tends to be an inverse relationship between companies that are in a glamorous industry and those that endure over the long term. Stanley and Danko (2010) refer to companies that are commonly owned by self-made millionaires and that perform well over time as "dull-normal".

Ruback and Yudkoff (2017) similarly note dull businesses to be terrific business opportunities as they are more likely to yield stable incomes over time. This is in part because "dull-normal industries don't attract a great deal of competition, and demand for their offerings is not usually subject to rapid downturns" (Stanley and Danko, 2010, p. 238).

I witnessed this in the restaurant industry. As trends in hospitality shifted, restaurant brands disappeared as fast as they emerged. Yet, many of their suppliers remained in business for years. The website of one of the major suppliers – a distributor of food safety products and systems, including leasing and maintenance of dishwashers – notes that it has been in business for over 100 years. Yet, how many restaurants do you know that have been in business anywhere near that long?

When considering the durability of a company, think about what trends could disrupt the industry and have a significant impact on the organization's profitability. Is this a business that will still be operational in 20 years, or is it serving a trend?

Choose your business wisely. Seek a business that will withstand the test of time. Following a trend may be successful for quick money, but a dull business, with stable cash flows for the long term, is more in line with building and retaining enduring wealth.

Recurring vs Nonrecurring Revenue

Stability of your revenue base is among the most important factors for ensuring the long-term viability of a company. Recurring revenue – as compared to nonrecurring – provides for assurances towards protecting your cash flow stream and thus your continued wealth.

Recurring revenue provides predictability and stability and tends to come in the form of contracts, subscriptions, or simply through customer loyalty.

Nonrecurring revenue is less predictable and thus less reliable.

An example of a nonrecurring revenue is when a company has to continually bid on jobs in order to secure short-term project revenue. If the business must constantly bid on the open market to maintain its current revenue base, the organization's revenue, and thus its cash flow stream, are constantly at risk.

A key determinant of the value of your business is the degree to which your customers are locked into your service continuously (Annis and Schine, 2015).

To examine the likelihood of customers switching from your company to another, you will want to examine a number of factors, including how long they have been purchasing from the company and the extent of switching costs. Switching costs include the costs of cancelling their service with you, searching for and sourcing out an alternative provider, examining a new provider's service rating and signing up with them.

Long-term contracts (provided they are high-margin contracts) provide more value to the company than short-term contracts or no contract at all, all else being equal. If you have to rebid at frequent intervals, there is a cost to retaining the customer and an ever-present reality of losing the customer.

It is important to constantly examine the extent of recurring vs nonrecurring revenue in your company, as an assessment of the vulnerability of your revenue stream. In most businesses, you can adjust your customer base towards a healthier proportion of recurrent clients, and in most cases, take steps towards increasing switching costs – whether that be contracting, subscriptions, reduced rates for loyalty or a good old fashioned high level of customer service.

Customer Concentration

Customer concentration is a measure of how revenue by individual customers is spread across the total revenue base. A low customer concentration occurs when multiple customers each contribute to a small portion of the company's total revenue, whereas a high customer concentration occurs when a small handful of customers make up a large portion of total revenue.

A low concentration is thus preferred. Companies with lower customer concentration are worth more due to a decrease in the consequence of flight risk; with a high customer concentration, a loss of one or two customers can have a significant impact, if not a crippling effect, on the viability of the business. While you may find synergies in serving fewer customers – e.g., streamlined communication, deeper relationships – the associated risks often outweigh the benefits.

Although business schools do teach the calculation of a customer concentration ratio, there is no magic formula in assessing acceptable levels. You will be required to use some logic in your risk assessment. What would happen to the company if the largest customer left? What about the top three customers? Would you still be able to manage your fixed costs and still be able to service the debt from the acquisition? Would your business still be a valuable asset to hold?

If your business has significantly high customer concentration, you do not have a business, you have a customer; you have a consulting job and not a business.

Some authors suggest that any individual "customer averaging over 10% of a company's sales is considered a red flag" (Annis and Schine, 2015, p. 242). In such instances, you should take action to manage that risk. For example, by growing the organization further, you are not only adding income to the organization, but also reducing risk as that customer becomes a smaller portion of your revenue.

The Fixed Cost vs Variable Cost Model

When examining the long-term viability of a company, it is important to understand the organization's vulnerability to revenue drops.

Fixed costs are expenses that do not fluctuate with changes in the level of output. Examples of fixed costs include office rent, term loans and management salaries. If you produce more or less units of output, such expenses remain the same.

Fixed cost models work well when there is a high level of certainty in your revenue stream. For example, if your contracts provide certainty. Fixed cost models also work well when the organization is growing because with each additional unit of production, the cost per unit decreases. Organizations operating in fixed cost industries may also be able to deter competition due to the high capital cost required for new entrants into the industry.

The challenge with high fixed costs is that the organization becomes vulnerable to drops in revenue. When sales decrease, the company can quickly find itself operating at a loss, unable to service its fixed costs.

This is common with storefront businesses, which have high rents as a large portion of their monthly expenditures. When there is an economic shift and they witness a revenue drop, they soon find themselves behind on their payment.

Companies operating on a variable cost model are better placed to react to changing environmental forces. Over the life of your business, it is important to constantly simulate scenarios of revenue decreases to examine what would occur to profitability. If you were to lose your three biggest clients, would you still be above a break-even net income?

Note that most businesses fall somewhere in the middle of the spectrum between fixed and variable cost businesses. It is also true that for many businesses, you are able to alter where the business falls along this spectrum by changing the structure of the largest expense items. For example, you could rent rather than buying select equipment.

If the fixed cost nature of your current business is creating a vulnerability to economic cycles, consider how you can apply these principles, ultimately converting select fixed cost line items to variable expenses.

STRUCTURING FOR ENDURANCE

Designing a Purposeful Life

By far, the biggest successes that I have achieved during my business tenure can be attributed back to one philosophy: Finding a better balance of thinking and doing.

Here it is. Step back from the day-to-day grind of your business. Take the time to read, learn and think. This allows you to build motivation, think big and think strategically. As a restaurant owner, on the floor every day taking orders and running food, how much thought are you giving to identifying customer trends? As a plumber, how much time are you devoting to meeting fellow business owners in an effort to acquire a neighbouring business?

Your focus should be on systems improvement, capital allocation, mentorship, identifying trends and making big-picture, strategic decisions. If you have a more complete view of the world around you, your one purposeful decision each month will provide better value to your business than making one hundred decisions daily – small choices that your empowered staff should be making. Train them, empower them and get out of their way.

Our current business took off the year I was focused on writing my first book. At the time, I had read well over 100 books in a year, sat on boards with people smarter than myself and was teaching at the local university.

These experiences gave me a very different lens on the world. A very different lens on our business than when I had previously been caught in the daily grind. I was feeding better knowledge and mentorship back to our business managers and better advice back to my business partners. Actions were purposeful and decisions were impactful.

Of course, I am not saying to ignore your business, abandon your staff, become disengaged or back off on your effort. In fact, I was putting in crazy hours. But the hours I was putting in were very purposeful.

You can choose how you do this – perhaps you go to the gym and then read for an hour every day. Is it newspapers, books or meeting with mentors? Find what works for you. Choose your own routine.

My contention is this: *Focus on what matters. Be informed about the world. Be purposeful in allocating your time. Be purposeful in designing your financial life. Be purposeful in designing your life.*

Business Insurance

Ensure your business is properly insured, including a general liability policy. Do not consider insurance as an expense, nor as a place where you can attempt to save money by taking the minimum coverage possible. Insurance is part of the required investment for conducting business. It is the necessary shield around your assets.

A few years after selling one of our restaurants, we were served with a lawsuit from a vehicle accident that had occurred five years earlier. We had been added as a third-party claimant to an ongoing dispute. A father of three children had, allegedly, left our restaurant intoxicated late at night, got into his company vehicle and proceeded to get into an accident at high speed and passed away.

The common law partner and the mother of the deceased each brought a suit against the employer and the motor vehicle insurance company for $2.2 million. The company holding the vehicle insurance later added us to the lawsuit, so we were on the hook to defend a claim for $2.2 million.

We had to defend this claim for three years! Do you know how much an insurance lawyer costs to employ for three years? Well, I now know how much. For three years, I had to compile document after document, attend questionings and witness some of the most heartbreaking testimony imaginable.

The end result? Eight years after the accident, our company was dropped from the lawsuit, because they had never attended our restaurant. They had the wrong restaurant. The passenger's story kept falling apart – an individual who was actually the driver and had lied about not driving. He had a long history of interactions with authority, jail and lying to the police.

Even if you are not at fault, litigation costs to defend a frivolous action can cripple your company and personal finances. A year's salary in legal bills to defend an incident that had absolutely nothing to do with us. I had never met them and they had never met me. They had never dealt with our company. Yet, there was an attempt to pierce the armour on a lifetime of earnings.

The good news: We had proper insurance coverage. Some would say we were over insured. Our business insurance covered our legal defence fees and, had they been at our restaurant, we had about six times this level of insurance coverage.

Properly planned insurance coverage can be your biggest ally for managing risk. Over your financial journey as an entrepreneur, you will inevitably become familiar with business insurance, automotive insurance, property insurance and life and disability insurance.

Protect your business. Proper levels of insurance are one factor in managing risk. You cannot build an Impenetrable Financial Legacy on a shaky foundation.

Business Dashboard

To grow and maintain wealth, you must never lose sight of the health of your business. Want to know the quickest way to bore a hole into your financial legacy? It's to not know what is going on in your business. If you do not know what is going on, you will be unable to correct your course before it is too late.

Every business requires a dashboard. A dashboard (often called a score card) is a set of numbers that you faithfully review periodically – either weekly or monthly, depending on the nature of your business – that provide the status of the health of your business.

Prior to creating a dashboard and determining what numbers are important to track, you must first know your core values, mission, vision and strategic plan. Such items must be completed in collaboration with staff. Only through collaboration will you achieve alignment and buy-in.

Most small businesses ignore strategic planning, dismissing it as a buzzword only applicable to large bureaucratic organizations. This is a mistake. Only by having a clearly articulated written path will you be able to achieve your organizational goals.

Strategic planning is a key determinant of organizational success, as it i) facilitates a conscious effort to review the external environment and assess internal strengths; ii) facilitates input and alignment from team members, enhancing their buy-in and thus accountability (e.g., higher enthusiasm and accountability for their piece of the dashboard) and iii) acts as a communication to external stakeholders as to what the organization stands for, ultimately leading to the self selection of customers that will be more aligned and stay for longer.

Strategic planning for small organizations does not need to be a formal or complicated process. If you do not have staff, it can be done by setting aside time for reflections and then writing down your goals. If you have a small team, it can be completed in an hour or two of dialogue and with a high-energy person in charge of a whiteboard.

You must then determine what you need to do now to achieve your long-term strategic plan – this is your dashboard. Your business will then run on a set of numbers that represent the health of the business. Determine what needs to be achieved in the short term in order to achieve the organization's long-term goals.

Such indicators must be leading indicators. Leading indicators are metrics that must be achieved in the near term (proactive) for the organization to achieve future desired outcomes. In contrast to lagging indicators, which are a measure of past results (reactive). The profitability of your organization would be a lagging indicator – by the time you can calculate your net income, it is too late to make any organizational changes to affect it.

As an example of a leading indicator, if you desire to increase net income by $50,000, working backwards, that might require $300,000 gross revenue, which may require 120 new clients. If your conversion rate is 20%, you will need 600 leads, or 50 leads per month. How do you get 50 more leads per month?

If your long-term goal is increased profits, you will require customer retention. Thus, understanding your customer service metrics would be a leading indicator of customer retention. While customer loss would be a lagging indicator. By the time you lost the customer, it is too late to take action.

Follow a similar exercise to determine what your leading indicators are.

Some months ago, we lost an administrator in our office, so I never received our dashboard for about four months. Once we got back on track, I was informed that we had lost a number of clients due to a shift in the economy.

What happens when you lose a client? Revenue goes down, net profit goes down and you are off track for wealth retention. Had I been receiving the dashboard, we would have caught the issues a number of steps before they led to the loss of a client. We would have caught them at the source, as leading indicators, before they translated into lost profits.

Never lose sight of the health of your business. Business is hard enough to make progress with external headwinds. Never allow controllable factors to move you backwards.

Choosing leading indicators means you do not have to wait until your year-end to know how your company is performing. By then, it is too late. Knowing early if you are off track allows you to proactively refocus efforts to get back on track.

Your dashboard must be achievable and completed in collaboration with the person responsible for achieving their individual metrics. Having such metrics also removes the subjectivity and emotions when discussing performance with team members, as conversations can focus on tangible results and how to achieve their numbers.

A Systems Approach

One of the best things you can do to protect your wealth is to scale your business. This comes with a huge disclaimer: When done properly. When you scale without structured systems, your profitability will inevitably work backwards. I know countless business owners who complain that after they grew their companies, they are putting in significantly more hours and are making less profit. Their businesses are in chaos.

Why? Because they are now numerous levels on the organizational chart removed from their staff and thus no longer have direct oversight on training, development, culture and process. They are relying on someone else to do the tasks they once completed themselves.

On the flip side, scaling, when done correctly, can be the most significant springboard ever imagined for building and protecting exponential wealth.

The timing of putting in place infrastructure is also a critical factor in your success. It is imperative to put it in place before growth, not during or after. This is a difficult concept for many operators who fail to comprehend the importance of planning and thus resist undertaking the significant upfront efforts. However, you need to stay ahead of the growth and plan the systems before you actually need them. Once you need them, once you witness errors in your system, including customer complaints, it is too late. Look at it as short-term pain for long-term gain.

In Michael Gerber's seminal book on taking a systems approach, he refers to the fact that "companies like McDonald's, Federal Express, and Disney didn't end up as mature companies. They started out that way! The people who started them had a totally different perspective about what a business is and why it works" (1995, p. 68). Act like you are a successful company and you will grow into your systems.

With growth comes energy, with energy comes innovation and with innovation comes a further capacity for growth. Your competitors are continually innovating and advancing alternative product solutions to your customer base. They are growing and achieving economies of scale, being able to offer more for less.

A major advantage that entrepreneurs have in building wealth is that, when set up correctly, your business should allow you to not be shackled to having to perform a certain task at a certain time of day to make a wage but rather to have the freedom to plan your own projects and the freedom and flexibility to participate in the activities of your choosing.

With respect to wealth building, you can spend time on big things, not small things: capital allocation, reading, thinking, planning, and working on the more productive aspects of your business. Hard work alone does not build wealth. For a business to provide that, it must not only provide a cash flow, but a cash flow that is not tied to your individual, hourly effort.

Michael Gerber popularized the systems approach as a conduit for growth as well as for removing yourself from the daily minutia, famously noting "[i]f your business depends on you, you don't own a business – you have a job. And it's the worst job in the world because you're working for a lunatic!" (1995, p. 40). The presupposition behind this is that you cannot achieve your overarching wealth objectives – however you choose to define them – by remaining an employee in your own business.

Only through scaling your newly acquired business can you scale your wealth. With an eye to wealth retention, it is imperative to prepare the business through a sequence of processes and systems.

Wealth from a business comes in the form of routine cash flow and the proceeds of a potential future sale. Wealth stability comes from building a moat around your company and putting up strategic guards against external forces that could threaten such future cash flow streams. Cash flow can be increased through growth, but just as importantly, must be protected by the same structured, systematic approach. Only through such an approach can wealth be retained.

Additionally, the future value of your business is increased and protected if your approach to growth has complied with the approach I present and, as advocated by others, in a way that allows the business to operate without being reliant on yourself or other key players. Only then will a future buyer have the confidence to pay for the value that you have created.

Simply put in place a series of processes ensuring every task is completed the same way every time, and in the way you expect it to be. No deviations, no misses, no mistakes.

Such systems ensure that while you grow, the following factors remain at the fore:

- Systems facilitate consistency of product or service delivery and reduce errors in process execution;
- Net income does not remain constant or decrease with growth but increases with efficiencies and economies of scale;
- The business is not reliant on yourself or key staff but on a sequence of replicable processes and systems;
- The business becomes a saleable asset whereby any potential buyers have assurance that the systems provide a safeguard to future cash flows.

With a systematized approach, the "system runs the business. The people run the system" (Gerber, 1995, p. 92). It is therefore the role of the owner and management "to develop those tools and to teach your people how to use them" (p. 101).

It is quite obvious now how systems can prevent errors – a task is completed the same way every time – and a product or service is provided to the customer the same way every time.

In working towards my first master's degree, I undertook a year-long research project that included travelling across Australia, interviewing organizations across various levels of the value chain. The efforts of this led me primarily to the conclusion that consistency trumps quality – something that McDonalds and Tim Hortons have known for many years.

Why are Tim Hortons and McDonald's so successful? It certainly is not due to the quality of their coffee or hamburgers! From a customer perspective, it is because of the predictability of their offering. It should not matter what location you go to, what time of day you arrive or who happens to be on shift at that particular time – the offering should be the same. The atmosphere is the same, the way you order is the same, and the product tastes the same and has the same texture, smell, and temperature. You know exactly what it will be like before you purchase it.

Business operators who are intentional about each process and the resulting outcome of each process witness success along with their growth. The alternative, which is not uncommon, is operators who let the business happen around them.

Although there are many ways to document operating procedures, the overarching approach is the same: Plan each step – whether that be customer interaction, hiring procedures, sequence of assembly or dress code – and document the most desirable way to perform such tasks for your specific organizational goals. Growth then becomes less risky because it does not matter if you have 10 or 10,000 customers, the process is the same.

Intentional About Growth

The company's workflow processes are then organized around business functions and systems and not around the owner or its key people (Gerber, 1995). If a team member were to quit, the business continues without missing a beat. If you, as the owner, take off for a month – for a vacation or to undertake due diligence on the next venture – the business not only chugs along but continues to grow, all while following the predetermined processes.

A significant portion of this philosophy is also rooted in being able to relinquish control and get out of the trenches, trusting that each task is performed in a way that you have predetermined to be the most effective.

Systems are not just documentation but comprise a plethora of comingled activities and paradigms, including technology, automation, control systems, process audits, culture and employee support systems. In this sense, every company should consider itself to be a technology company. No matter what your product is, there should be a continual examination of increased efficiency and automation.

In this sense, success in entrepreneurship "has less to do with what's done in a business and more to do with how it's done. The commodity isn't what's important – the way it's delivered is" (Gerber, 1995, p. 73). For example, Amazon is not a bookseller but a technology company with an expertise in automation of distribution. Uber is not a transportation company but a technology company that has harnessed a reliable automation process projected to the world as a mobile software application.

It matters less what you do and more how you do it. Where do your skills lie? Not in cooking, mechanics or some other job skill, but in distribution, sales or manufacturing automation. It is the latter that will define the success of your company.

"A business can fail in two ways: not surviving beyond its start and not reaching its full potential. While shutdowns receive the most attention, failure to reach full potential is much more catastrophic" (Johnson, 2013, p. 15). Systematize your business as a prerequisite to growth. And only then will you be able to scale your wealth to new heights. Such an approach to growth, controlling every business process, is likened to placing a moat around your wealth, protecting it from external forces.

Note that much of the content in this section has been adapted from my first book, *Faster Safer Wealthier*.

Summary

As an entrepreneur, you have a great tailwind that is unavailable to the nine-to-fivers. You have a business with the potential to feed you an income, month after month, year after year, all while it grows in value. An asset that pays dividends and appreciates in value.

The value that any one individual can extract from a nine-to-five job is capped by the formula of wage multiplied by the number of hours worked. And there is only so much you can alter these two variables.

Unlike a nine-to-five job, the growth in income and value of a business is not capped. With care and attention, the asset will provide cash flow to feed your index investing and real estate down payments.

To ensure that the business is a conduit for long-term wealth, you must not only own an enduring business but also ensure that such factors remain. You must think like both an entrepreneur and an investor. You must continually monitor the internal innerworkings – keeping an eye on your dashboard and maintaining a systems approach, as well as ensuring your knowledge of external forces. Your efforts must remain focused on strategic thinking.

The lessons prescribed here are not just about building your business, but most importantly about preserving its value.

However, a successful multi-million dollar exit of your business is not guaranteed. Would you put your family's whole life savings into one stock? I think not. Yet, this is what almost all business owners do, placing their whole net worth into their business. A downturn, an illness, a divorce, overleveraging, a shift in consumer trends – any one of these can lead to complete devastation of your finances, having to start from zero.

That strategy doesn't sound like an astute investor to me. It sounds more like an all-in Vegas red or black gamble.

You must own assets in the three asset classes prescribed here. You must think like both an entrepreneur and an investor. You are the CEO of your family office. Be intentional in securing your family wealth for the long term.

REFERENCES

Annis, David and Gary Schine. *Strategic Acquisition: A Smarter Way to Grow a Business*, 2nd edition. Sandra Publications, 2015.

Bott, Gregory. *Faster Safer Wealthier: Skip the Start-up and Buy a Stable Business to Build Intergenerational Wealth*. Abja Inc, 2021.

Gerber, Michael E. *The E-Myth Revisited: Why Most Small Businesses Don't Work and What to Do About It*. HarperCollins Publishers, 1995.

Johnson, Kevin D. *The Entrepreneur Mind: 100 Essential Beliefs, Characteristics, and Habits of Elite Entrepreneurs*. Johnson Media Inc., 2013.

Ruback, Richard S. and Royce Yudkoff. *HBR Guide to Buying a Business: Think big, Buy small, Own your own company*. Harvard Business Review Press, 2017.

Stanley, Thomas J., and William D. Danko. *The Millionaire Next Door: The Surprising Secrets of America's Wealthy*. Taylor Trade Publishing, 2010.

Asset Two: Own a Piece of Every Business

Five

INDEX FUNDS

Your business is complicated, stressful and all-consuming. Your life and your portfolio would not be sustainable if your other assets took up as much time as your business. Enter index funds – the simplest asset you never knew you needed.

Many people think picking stocks is the way to invest in the stock market. Perhaps it is the feeling of being in control, or the adrenaline that comes with the possibility of an upside if they were to choose the right stock – an attempt to replicate the windfall of a lottery winner – or maybe it is simply the only way that they have been taught and have come to understand as the most familiar route to investing.

Entrepreneurs, by definition, like to control their investments, so it is no surprise that they exemplify this philosophy.

The problem is "that 75% of all of the smartest money managers in the world, working 20 hour days, with huge research staffs, powered by the most advanced computers, have not been able to consistently beat the market. Of the remaining 25 percent, most were just able to keep pace with the market (but when you factor in commissions and fees you're still a net loser)" (Allen, 2000, p. 51).

DOI: 10.4324/9781003724247-5

Yet, with historical returns of around 11%, the stock market remains a great place to invest.

How to Ensure Market Returns

A consistent 11% on my investments sounds pretty good to me. So how does one ensure market returns? By buying the whole market.

This logic takes us to purchasing groupings of stocks, of which there are two overarching choices: mutual funds or index funds. There are two reasons why I resonate more with the literature that suggests index funds over salespeople who recommend mutual funds.[1]

Reason one: Index funds tend to outperform mutual funds.

Mutual funds are actively managed and their performance is based on the individual stocks that a fund manager chooses to include. While well researched and intended, their track record is still subordinate to the overarching market, especially when accounting for fees to manage the fund. Fees can have a significant long-term effect on your investment's ability to compound wealth over time.

"In short, mutual funds are prevalent because of their convenience, but because actively managed mutual funds are, by definition, expensive, they're not the best investment anymore. Active management can't compete with passive management, which takes us to index funds, the more attractive cousin of mutual funds" (Sethi, 2019, p. 234).

Reason two: Management fees are more expensive with mutual funds than with index funds, which can have a significant long-term impact on the growth of your portfolio.

When choosing an index fund, you must also be conscious of management fees (expense ratio), which should play a factor in the decision of the fund that you choose.

The Success and Simplicity of Index Funds

In favour of index funds, JL Collins notes "from January 1975–January 2015 [...] the market returned an average of 11.9% per year ... the actual returns for any given year were all over the place. But when the dust settled, over that 40-year period, the average was 11.9%. That is a breathtaking number" (Collins, 2016, p. 15).

With a long enough timeframe to compound wealth with market returns, you will be in the minority of people who will be prepared for retirement. It is quite easy to do. But the problem is that it is also quite easy not to do.

Numerous authors of personal finance literature point to the fact that, over time, buying a bundle of stocks that are intended to mimic the overall market outperform those who spend copious amounts of time researching and buying individual stocks. There are numerous reasons for this:

- Transaction costs of continually buying and selling stocks add up and take away from the possible return. When hiring a professional money manager, this is compounded by the cost they charge to actively manage your funds;
- There are simply too many variables in modern society, including global events and economic swings, that can affect individual stocks;
- It is nearly impossible to have an information advantage when trading in public sector stocks. The news you read is available to millions of others;
- There is a human tendency to react to the market incorrectly and abruptly. If a stock goes down, individuals panic and sell. When working with a more macro-outlook of investing in the whole market, there is a greater realization of the importance of dollar cost averaging and

an understanding that lows create opportunities to purchase more stocks (they become on sale so that you can purchase more with your monthly allotment). You can have greater confidence that your bundle of stocks will recover because the market always has, and you have bought into the market. With individual stocks, it can be harder to separate the reasoning behind the drops and thus difficult to determine whether the individual stock will recover;

- One argument with individual stock picking is that the investor is trying to determine which small-cap companies will be their home run investment. But with buying individual stocks, you are buying into fewer companies and are very unlikely to determine which specific companies will be winners. When you buy into the market, the home runs will still be in your bundle 20 years from now, as they will still be listed on the exchange and included in your chosen fund;
- As an entrepreneur, your time is precious. Seemingly paradoxical, the less time you spend moving stocks in and out of your portfolio, the better your returns.

When to Invest in Index Funds

Stick with it for the long run, through both the highs and lows. Just keep allocating a portion of your monthly salary to your investment account and keep buying every month for the long run.

In his book, *The Intelligent Investor*, Benjamin Graham defines dollar cost averaging as: "simply that the practitioner invests in common stock the same number of dollars each month or each quarter. In this way he buys more shares when the market is low than when it is high, and he is likely to end up with a satisfactory overall price for all his holdings" (2003, p 29).

"With dollar cost averaging, you don't have to be smart. You can be a total idiot and still win. You just buy every month. You buy during the good times. You buy during the bad times. You don't care what the headlines are saying" (Allen, 2000, p. 58). "Ironically, a crash at the beginning of your investing life is a gift. In fact, any pullback in stock prices is a gift while you are in the process of accumulating your wealth. It allows you to buy more shares for your dollars, on sale if you will" (Collins, 2016, p. 81).

Consistent with the theme in this book of never lose money, while every investor will desire to attain a better result than the overall market, the intelligent investor must first "make sure that his results will not be worse. It is no difficult trick to bring a great deal of energy, study, and native ability into Wall Street and to end up with losses instead of profits" (Graham, 2003, p. 29).

Charlie Munger has been quoted as saying "The first rule of compounding is to never interrupt it unnecessarily" (Pape, 2022, p. 153). Just keep buying, not panicking in the downturns.

No Compromises to Monthly Investing

Personal finance gurus suggest investing 10–20% of your monthly earnings, while some authors, such as JL Collins, encourage saving up to 50% of your earnings (yes, I know people who do this). He suggests that if you start early with a lower percentage, when you obtain raises over the course of your career, do not let lifestyle inflation creep into your spending. Rather, by continuing to live on a similar amount and investing any raises that you obtain (or a portion thereof), you will quickly reach up towards that 50%.

Building wealth is simple. It is about developing good financial habits and repeating them over and over for an extended period of time.

Next, automate your financial goals.

To ensure consistent contributions, automating your wealth generation is a must. Without automation, human nature is prone to making excuses to skip a month, which can then lead to a number of months. There will always be a "valid" reason not to contribute to your future self, as a reaction to something in your personal or business life that seems important in the moment.

So set up an automatic transfer coming out of your daily bank account into your TFSA (Tax Free Savings Account) and RRSP (Registered Retirement Savings Plan) accounts. Once the funds are in these tax-efficient accounts, you can then place your order to purchase your index funds. More details on this below.

Having your wealth generation on autopilot removes the discretion that can be overturned by the temptation of immediate gratification. You do not require a budget and you do not have to be disciplined; it just happens, automatically, every month, month after month, year after year.

Be Intentional About Your Destination

While there is a science to how personal finance authors and scholars have arrived at the above percentages, there are also a lot of personal variables that come into play, which negate the usefulness of rule-of-thumb numbers.

I am a believer in starting with the end goal in mind and then determining how to best achieve such an outcome. First, determine the asset value you require at retirement to produce your desired income. Then, use an online calculator to determine how much you need to invest each month to achieve that goal.

If you are a business owner in your fifties or older, you may wish to examine your other assets and choose whether index funds are supplementary to your retirement or your whole retirement. For example, if your other assets have certainty of providing 40% of your required retirement, then index funds will need to make up the 60% shortfall.

For everyone else that either has a longer runway or the ability to put in the required monthly contributions, I suggest contributing to the level that index funds make up the full amount required to retire. It would be a perfectly fine problem to have too much money to give away, to continue to invest and to contribute to your purpose during retirement. After all, this book isn't about survival at retirement. It is about building substantial and sustainable wealth that continues to grow into your retirement and beyond your life.

My wish for you is to be able to retire from the cash flow of your business (either through the income or from the sale of your business), retire fully from your real estate holdings and fully off your index funds. Each of the three asset classes are significant and will continue to produce. You will have built up a large enough base that you can live off the proceeds and drawing down on the base isn't even a consideration.

I have only provided a brief overview of personal finance to convince you of the one area of your life where you need to think like an employee. I suggest reading JL Collins's book, *The Simple Plan to Wealth*, to learn more about why index funds are the best bet for retirement, and Ramit Sethi's book, *I Will Teach You to be Rich*, for a step-by-step execution on how to manage your personal finances and automate your index fund investing to retire rich.

Asset Allocation Within Your Index Funds

For the nine-to-fiver, as you approach retirement, you must shift more and more towards an asset allocation that favours certainty. Such individuals have been advised to shift towards an increased allocation of fixed income and away from growth stocks, as they do not have the cushion to withstand market fluctuations.

If you have built up just enough to sneak through retirement, there is no cushion for market fluctuations. For these individuals, this makes perfect sense. But with this comes the inevitable trade-off of a low return.

For the average person, it therefore becomes prudent to start to shift their allocation in their thirties and continue to do so up until retirement, at which point a significant portion of their portfolio is gaining little returns – in the name of safety – with only about half of the portfolio in equities. Predictability is essential.

For these individuals, this is a must. What if the stock market crashes when you are 65? Would you be forced to return to work? Would your health permit you to work? Would your kids be forced to sacrifice their retirement to assist with yours?

If you have diversification within your index funds and the three asset classes as suggested throughout this book, you do not have to be as conservative as most personal finance authors would suggest.

Many parts of the tax structure that we are most familiar with have been set up to transfer the wealth of the nine-to-fiver to the government in the form of taxation. Some of this is unavoidable. For example, you will be forced to draw down on your RRSP and pay taxes on it.

The astute entrepreneur can protect their family wealth during taxation triggers, such as retirement and death. Life insurance, trusts and lifetime capital gains exemptions are some of the most beneficial and effective items in the income tax act of most jursidictions, including the Income Tax Act in Canada. Speak to your accountant about these and many other ways to protect your wealth.

You Have Earned the Right to Continue to Earn

None of this applies to you. Your wealth is higher. Your goals are different. You have earned the right to continue to accumulate wealth.

You will have massive wealth: Your index funds will be across all sectors and not reliant on a single stock or single industry; your business will have a risk mitigation strategy, as presented in previous chapters, set up to withstand severe storms; and you will own multiple asset classes that are uncorrelated. For you, there is a fortress around your empire that others do not have.

As an astute entrepreneur, developing an Impenetrable Financial Legacy, with assets across index funds, real estate and your business, you have the luxury of continuing to grow your net worth during retirement and not to draw down on it. You can set your target date funds to a later date. You can keep your emerging market funds. You do not have to convert high-growth funds into fixed income.

Investment adviser, Ashby Daniels, articulates: "When investing for retirement and our children's education, I will excitedly say that our portfolio is 100% equities. Some might say this is foolish and that we should own some percentage of fixed income to reduce the volatility of the portfolio, but I disagree because we have no short-term goals. It is widely accepted that anything that reduces short-term volatility must also reduce long-term risk. Given this fact, it seems illogical to own anything but equities assuming we have the emotional fortitude to think truly long term. I believe we do and will continue to own 100% equities" (Daniels, in Brown and Portnoy, 2020, p. 97).

And equities have outperformed other market assets time and time again when examining a long enough time horizon. They outperform bonds, most commodities, real estate investment trusts, guaranteed investment certificates and pretty much everything else.

What Type of Equities Should I Hold?

But what type of equities should you hold? Examples of equity themes within index funds include domestic equities, developed world equities and emerging market equities. And you can further dissect your choices into sector themes, such as health care, energy, information technology, financial and companies with a strong environmental, social and governance focus. And what about large-cap, mid-cap and small-cap companies?

You really only require one index fund, if it has your desired growth prospects, diversification (e.g., sector, region) and risk tolerance (currency, political, regional). Even domestic funds include large-cap stocks that have a significant portion of their business activities in international markets.

If you want to have some further command over your allocation, as I do for myself, you may want to choose a number of index funds in an effort to find your personal preferences.

Your ideal allocation will include domestic and international funds, some of which are high growth, being cognizant of exposure to international currencies as most international funds are bought and sold in US dollars.

With the dominance of the US financial sector, it can be a challenge to adequately diversify away from US stocks and funds in US dollars. However, the challenge is not insurmountable. It is important for those not living in the US to have a keen sense of their exposure to all international currencies, with a particular cognizance of not having complete exposure to US dollars.

For example, you may wish to have a high weighting in a total market index in a domestic fund (diversified, reduced currency risk, mirrors the inflation of your local market) and a certain allocation towards developed world international large-cap and exposure to both large-cap and small-cap within emerging markets across more than one region. A portfolio of index funds of this nature may contain around 4–6 index funds, each with a different allocation within the respective fund.

However, it is important not to lose sight of the overarching objective of index funds. Research suggests that most educated and active stock pickers cannot routinely beat the returns of buying the whole market. Logic then follows that it becomes counterproductive to have more than a very small handful of index funds and to not allocate too heavily towards a specific sector or region. You must therefore lean towards buying the whole market.

The wealthy think in 100-year cycles. Their goal is to continue to grow their family wealth during their senior years and not to draw down on it. When you view your holdings as a family office – an entity that will continue throughout generations – your personal retirement is not a trigger to change course as it would be for others.

When you are 70, your kids, nieces and nephews may only be 40 and their kids may be very young. And their kids not yet born. When viewing your wealth as a family office and not your personal retirement, it makes more sense to continue to compound wealth, always. I have never read this advice in any finance literature. Personal finance writers are unequivocally focused on building an industry whereby life stages trigger shifts in asset reallocation, ultimately creating the need for new financial products.

Simply shift the philosophy of your net worth being your personal wealth, to a philosophy of family wealth, whereby you are simply the custodian of it for future generations.

TAX-ADVANTAGED VEHICLES

Registered Retirement Savings Plan (RRSP)

To maximize the growth of your assets and preserve the value of your empire, you must utilize tax-efficient vehicles to the full extent possible. In the context of index funds, this means first purchasing them inside of tax-advantaged investment vehicles of RRSPs and TFSAs before then investing any overflow in non-tax-advantaged accounts.

While the following sections focus on examples from the Canadian tax mechanisms, most developed economies have similar schemes available as an incentive for the population to save for retirement.

The government of Canada defines a Registered Retirement Savings Plan (RRSP) as a "retirement savings plan that you establish with an issuer, that the CRA registers, and to which you or your spouse or common-law partner contribute. Deductible RRSP contributions can be used to reduce your tax. Any income you earn in the RRSP is usually exempt from tax as long as the funds remain in the plan. You generally have to pay tax when you receive payments from the plan" (Canada Revenue Agency, accessed 2024).

An RRSP is thus a "program designed to encourage Canadians to save for retirement by providing tax deductions for contributions and tax-sheltered growth for earnings inside the plan" (Pape, 2014, p. 25). With an RRSP, you receive a tax deduction at your current marginal tax rate when you contribute to the plan, and income earned within your RRSP can grow tax-free for as long as the funds remain within the RRSP.

For example, if your marginal tax rate is 30% and you contribute $10,000 to your RRSP in a given period, you have a tax deduction (money back into your pocket to reinvest) of $3,000. This is an instant 30% return on your money, which is nothing short of an amazing return on your investment. If you then decide to invest these savings, you have a 30% higher principal base working for you.

You are not required to take the deduction in the same year as you make your contribution. Therefore, if your current income is low – e.g., just starting a business, you have other deductions such as university tuition, or a leave of absence – and is planned to be increased in the coming years, you can defer your deduction to be claimed during a year where your marginal tax rate will be higher, whereby you will receive a larger deduction.

It is best to not stop contributions in lower tax rate years as the sooner your investment starts to work for you, the better. You do not want to lose momentum once you have established the discipline to invest. Alternatively, in such years, you have the option of redirecting such funds into your TFSA, still maintaining investment momentum.

Note that an RRSP is not an investment, but rather a tax-advantaged investment vehicle. You don't simply transfer money into an RRSP and let it sit. You must take the next step and place it within a permitted investment. Permitted investments within an RRSP include money and deposits of either domestic or foreign currency; listed securities, shares of public corporations, mutual funds, bonds, among numerous other investments and, yes, index funds!

When you decide to make a withdrawal from your RRSP account, you pay taxes on the amount withdrawn at your then current marginal tax rate.

The amount that you can contribute to your RRSP is calculated as the amount carried forward from previous years, plus the lesser of 18% of your earned income in the previous year and the annual RRSP limit (which was $30,780 for 2023).

You can contribute to your RRSP until December 31st of the year you turn 71, as long as you have an available deduction limit.

You can contribute to an RRSP – yours, your spouse's or your common-law partner's RRSP – up to the end of February of the following tax calendar year end. However, it is best to contribute monthly. Contributing monthly will give you a higher return as monthly contributions will start to compound earlier than contributions occurring at the end of the year. Automated monthly contributions also remove the need to be disciplined, ensuring that you stay on track. You can certainly top up your total contributions at year end.

During a recent vacation, one high-earning couple that I met had withdrawn from their RRSPs to attend the vacation. That was dumb. It is especially important not to interrupt your RRSP account by withdrawing during your working tenure, especially during high-earning years, when your marginal tax rate is high.

Withdrawing your RRSP attacks your wealth in many ways. It immediately decreases your net worth, as the withdrawal is taxed at your marginal rate. The funds are removed from your net worth and disappear into the darkness of consumer spending. The withdrawal further decreases your future earnings potential as those funds, when withdrawn for consumer expenditures, are no longer contributing to your future wealth. And you do not get that RRSP room back for future use.

Charlie Munger has been quoted as saying: "The first rule of compounding is to never interrupt it unnecessarily" (Pape, 2022, p 153). Just keep buying, not panicking in the downturns.

Housel similarly notes that compounding "doesn't rely on earning big returns. Merely good returns sustained uninterrupted for the longest period of time – especially in times of chaos and havoc – will always win" (Housel, 2020, p. 63).

Investing inside a tax-advantaged account, such as an RRSP, is a great tool for wealth accumulation and you are doing yourself a disservice if you are not capturing the benefits. Make sure you are maxing out your allowable contribution room every year.

Tax Free Savings Account (TFSA)

Unlike an RRSP, contributions to a TFSA (Tax Free Savings Account) are not tax-deductible. The account holder contributes after-tax dollars to their TFSA account, but any amount contributed as well as any income earned on the investments held within the account is tax-free upon withdrawal.

Your contribution room increases by a prescribed amount each year, which is not contingent on your earned income. The annual TFSA contribution limit started at $5,000 in 2009 and is indexed to inflation, with 2026 providing for a TFSA contribution limit of $7,000.

Your total available contribution room is calculated as the total TFSA dollar limit for the current year, plus any unused contribution room carried forward from previous years, plus any withdrawals made from the TFSA in the previous year.

If you withdraw funds in the current year, you do not lose the contribution room, as it is added back to your limit the following year. This is not the case for an RRSP.

You are the only one who can make contributions or withdrawals to your TFSA. However, given that contributions are after-tax dollars (meaning that the government does not lose any immediate revenue from a contribution), you are able to provide cash to others, such as a spouse, so that they can contribute directly to their own TFSA.

As with an RRSP, a TFSA is simply an investment vehicle and not an investment. Once funds are transferred into your TFSA, you have the option of how to invest those funds. Permitted investments include cash, mutual funds, securities listed on a designated stock exchange, index funds, guaranteed investment certificates, bonds and certain shares of small business corporations. Such qualified investments are similar to those that are allowed within an RRSP.

A TFSA is an Extremely Valuable Tool for Building and Retaining Wealth

Most sources of wealth that one accumulates during their lifetime are heavily taxed when you decide to access them during retirement. The sale of real estate, withdrawals of RRSPs, sale of your business (once you exceed the limit of your lifetime capital gains exemption), gains on the sale of shares not held within tax-exempt vehicles and almost every other investment that builds wealth are subject to heavy taxation when accessed. And taxation directly and significantly reduces wealth.

It is therefore beneficial to have assets that have grown over time that are not taxed upon liquidation. Not only do you retain the full value of them, but the extra value as a result provides a friendly offset against the tax liability of your taxable assets. For example, proceeds from a TFSA can be a source for paying off the tax liability upon the disposition of a rental property.

It is also important to note that since TFSA withdrawals are not considered as income, income earned within a TFSA or a withdrawal of your TFSA does not trigger a claw back of government retirement safety nets such as the Guaranteed Income Supplement and Old Age Security, or a reduction in employment income benefits.

Unlike an RRSP, you do not receive a tax deduction from the contribution, as you deposit after-tax dollars into a TFSA. The idea is that both the original principal and any income accumulated inside of a TFSA can be withdrawn at any time without any taxation.

The name TFSA is a bit misleading. As a retirement vehicle, it should be used as an investment tool and not a savings tool. While you can hold assets such as cash or guaranteed income certificates inside your TFSA, you would be missing out on the tax advantages from doing so. What you want to hold within a TFSA are assets that have growth potential over time and provide the best return within your risk tolerance.

If you hold significant cash balances or low-return assets within your TFSA, such deposits use up contribution room that could be utilized in gaining tax-free returns.

When to Use a TFSA vs an RRSP

The general rule is as follows: "If you expect your tax rate after retirement to be the same as it is now, TFSAs and RRSPs will produce the same net result. If you expect your tax rate after retirement to be less than it is now, top up your RRSP before opening a TFSA. If you expect your tax rate after retirement to be higher than it is now, saving in a TFSA will produce a better return than making an RRSP contribution" (Pape, 2009, p. 47).

Many business owners at the start of their career will be able to keep their personal taxable income low, as excess earnings will be kept inside the company at a lower tax rate than their personal marginal tax bracket. Therefore, the tax deduction from an RRSP will be lower than the tax liability upon withdrawing that same investment and earned income during retirement. In such instances, aggressive contributions to your TFSA in early years will make more sense.

When following the wealth-building formula described in this book, upon retirement, you will have multiple assets that have accumulated in value. Unfortunately, most of them will cause tax liabilities when accessed. Therefore, a TFSA should be a significant tool to fully utilize.

Regardless of your tax bracket and the intricacies of choosing between a TFSA and an RRSP, such tax-advantaged tools should be heavily utilized and, whenever possible, to the maximum allowable contribution limit.

They each provide for significant tax advantages, contributing to wealth accumulation and preservation. For those who start their investment journey early in life, they will certainly reach the contribution limits of both of these vehicles. Only then do you start to invest outside of tax-advantaged investment accounts.

Ensure both you and your spouse are maxing out tax-sheltered vehicles, which may require contributions to each other's RRSPs and TFSAs from time to time. And confirm you are listed on each other's plans as the beneficiary to ensure a smooth transition upon death.

Chapter Summary

A consistent and disciplined approach is to relentlessly invest every month without compromise. Doing so within tax-efficient accounts helps to not only continue to build wealth but to also retain wealth. While this alone will be enough to build significant wealth and financial freedom into retirement, it is still only one piece of the larger personal strategic plan for an astute entrepreneur looking to build an Impenetrable Financial Legacy.

With sufficient holdings, in conjunction with your business and real estate, you will be able to maintain a growth philosophy and continue to accept market returns in the transition of wealth between generations, and not have to reallocate toward a low-risk/low-return fixed income instrument, sacrificing wealth building out of necessity of having to quasi-freeze your estate for fears of a market drop just before or during retirement.

Most people build for 30 years, preserve it for 10, and then tear it down for 30 years. What would happen if you now had 70 years of wealth building? That is a huge window through which to continue to build intergenerational wealth. If you plan for your estate to continue beyond your time on earth, why stall its growth between the ages of 50 and 90?

NOTE

1 Note that when I refer to index funds moving forward, I am referring to a grouping of stocks that are intended to replicate the performance of a select market and are passively managed exchange traded funds with low expense ratios that are not inside of a mutual fund.

REFERENCES

Allen, Robert. *Multiple Streams of Income: How to Generate a Lifetime of Unlimited Wealth*. John Wiley & Sons, 2000.

Canada Revenue Agency. "Registered Retirement Savings Plan (RRSP)." Government of Canada. Last modified (February 2, 2025). https://www.canada.ca/en/revenue-agency/services/tax/individuals/topics/registered-retirement-savings-plan-rrsp.html. (Accessed 23 March, 2026).

Collins, JL. *The Simple Path to Wealth: Your Road Map to Financial Independence and a Rich, Free Life*. JL Collins, 2016.

Daniels, Ashby. "Ashby Daniels." In *How I Invest My Money: Finance Experts Reveal How They Save, Spend, and Invest*, edited by Joshua Brown and Brian Portnoy. Harriman House Ltd, 2020.

Graham, Benjamin. *The Intelligent Investor: A Book of Practical Council, Revised Edition*. HarperCollins Publishers Inc, 2003.

Housal, Morgan. *The Psychology of Money: Timeless Lessons on Wealth, Greed, and Happiness*. Harriman House Ltd, 2020.

Pape, Gordon. *Tax-Free Savings Accounts: A Guide to TFSAs and How They Can Make You Rich*. Penguin Group, 2009.

Pape, Scott. *The Barefoot Investor: The only Money Guide You'll Ever Need*. John Wiley & Sons Australia Ltd, 2022.

Sethi, Ramit. *I Will Teach You to be Rich: No Guilt. No Excuses. No BS. Just a 6-Week Program That Works. Second Edition*. Workman Publishing Co., 2019.

Asset Three: Real Estate

Six

STRATEGIC REAL ESTATE AND YOU

Real estate is a great complementary asset class for entrepreneurs to own. While businesses tend to be a cash flow game, real estate is an equity game. Businesses provide a cash flow stream for the owner, which not only provides them with a personal income but is a mechanism for the accumulation of other assets, such as real estate.

My approach to real estate as an asset class in an entrepreneur's portfolio follows some overlapping characteristics of index funds: I suggest buying high-quality properties slowly over time. This strategy is achievable, safe and extremely impactful on your net worth over the long term.

Many new investors attend courses and come home with the inspirational goal of accumulating a target number of properties, an extreme number of which has been taught to them. A fixation on the gross value of your holdings can lead to a mentality of risking what you already own and need for retirement. Such an aggressive presupposition can create too high an exposure to fluctuations in interest rates and result in an overallocation of real estate as a percentage of your holdings.

This initial fixation misses the point of what you are trying to achieve with real estate. The goal is not to add risk to your portfolio, but to add a stable asset class that complements

DOI: 10.4324/9781003724247-6

your business ownership, keeps pace with inflation and consistently adds to your net worth year after year.

Taking a conservative approach to real estate can have a significant impact on your net worth and retirement capacity. For example, if you require an additional $1.5 million to retire (e.g $60,000 per year following the 4% rule) and the average price of a single-family home in your area is $478,000 (the Canadian Real Estate Association reports the average sale of a single-family detached property to be $478,000 at the time of writing), then you would require the equivalent of just over three debt free properties before retirement.

If you wish to add more, that is great. But my point is that a conservative and very easily obtainable strategy can have a major impact on your net worth. While real estate can never be a truly passive strategy, even with the help of a property manager, a small portfolio of high-quality properties can be managed with very little effort and time.

You will be required to conduct a lot of research to develop your strategy, understanding areas within a city and defining your niche asset class. But once you are up and running, this approach does not require a huge time drain.

If real estate is not your passion or your daily business and is simply a means for wealth development, then accumulating a modest number of properties to supplement your portfolio will more than suffice. If you want to create a business around real estate, then you have the opportunity to learn more investment strategies to acquire a larger portfolio and cash stream.

An Example

Let me walk you through a recent example of a single-family property I purchased in Edmonton, Alberta, a few years back.

The property was listed for $265,000 and after some easy negotiations, I purchased it for $247,500.

In the environment at the time, properties above $350,000 were hard to generate positive or even break-even cash flow, as the carrying costs on them were too high in relation to rent values. And properties below a certain value were hard to obtain a strong tenant profile. A weaker tenant profile increases the likelihood of property damage, late rent, increased vacancy costs and an overall increased level of time and effort required to manage the property.

I happened to find a property that I felt was undervalued. It was in an average area and would show quite well to prospective tenants.

I chose to live in the property and put ten per cent down on it. This triggered a $13,000 mortgage insurance premium, giving a starting mortgage balance of $235,750. It would have been wise to provide a 20% down payment on the property to avoid this mortgage premium.

I eventually moved out of the property and converted it into a rental property. My monthly principal and interest payments totalled $1,084, monthly property taxes of $110, insurance premiums of $125, plus an allowance for vacancies and repairs and optional property management. The tenants paid the utilities and there are no condo fees on this property. The house was rented for $1,550 per month, which was essentially a break-even cash flow on a monthly and annual basis.

In five years, the mortgage balance went from $235,750 to $196,000, creating a net worth increase of $39,750. The property value also increased from the purchase price of $247,500 to $320,000, creating a further net worth increase of $72,500. If I were to sell this property at the end of the five-year mortgage term, I would put $124,000 cash in my pocket. Subtracting the original down payment, this gives a cash on cash return of 80% ($124,000 – $24,750 / $24,750 = 400 % / 5 years = 80% return per annum). Of course, there are realtor fees and closing costs, but you get the general picture.

But why sell? When you continue to hold onto the property, not only does appreciation continue to contribute to your net worth, but cash flow increases over time, as your mortgage continues at a relatively stable rate, but rental prices increase with inflation.

Some properties work out better, some worse. But they all have the same theme, whereby the typical net worth advantages with residential real estate are based on three pillars: appreciation, cash flow, and mortgage paydown.

Appreciation

The beauty of appreciation is that the total property appreciates, not simply your down payment. For example, if you put a 20% down payment on a property and that property appreciates by 3% per year, you have a 15% cash on cash return on your money. This is the power of leverage. If you own three average single-family properties, at a $478,000 value each, your net worth increases by $43,000 per year simply by holding onto these properties.

So appreciation alone, on three properties, is pushing towards the value of the average salary of an individual in Canada.

How do the strategic and disciplined get richer? This is how.

And the best part about appreciation is that it is tax-deferred. Like a tax-advantaged vehicle, such as an RRSP, you do not pay taxes on the appreciation until there is a trigger event, such as a sale or transfer of that asset. The tax authority does not require mark-to-market, whereby you report the value of the asset and include the increase in value as taxable income.

The appreciation generated by the investment vehicle continues to accumulate tax-free until some future event, such as the sale of the property.

Cash Flow

Many authors writing on residential real estate have a fixation on positive cash flow, placing all other variables as secondary. Real estate gurus tend to place such an emphasis on cash flow because real estate is their business. They require the cash as their source of living, so shift focus away from the other two variables and onto cash flow. And without a cash-flowing business independent of their real estate holdings, such emphasis on cash flow is required as a risk mitigation strategy.

Positive cash flow is important for many reasons. If you are having to inject money into your property bank account each month, you may lose motivation with sticking with your real estate journey, even if the other elements of your property continue to increase your net worth each month.

When you plan the real estate purchasing decisions around positive cash flow, and the unexpected occurs, such as increased periods of vacancy, unexpected repairs or increased interest rates, the unexpected pressures on cash flow might take a positive cash flow to a break-even or to a slightly negative cash flow. However, if you build your investment around negative cash flows, the unexpected can cause significant pressures.

One of the most important reasons to plan for positive cash flow is that a net loss on multiple properties is not sustainable and you will not be able to scale your portfolio, as each additional property will put more and more cash flow pressure on you. And financing of future properties will be a challenge, as you will not be able to show banks that you have a margin of safety to consistently meet any debt-service obligations.

Why work hard in other areas of your life, creating efficiencies in your business simply to inject it in to subsidizing a secondary asset class?

However, the challenge with cash flow is that with residential real estate, there is often a negative correlation between cash flow and appreciation potential. Return on investment calculation is based on both a numerator and a denominator – return (cash flow plus appreciation) divided by the cost of the investment.

When you find a cheap property (reducing your cost of investment) in a rough area and rent it out, or a cheap wooden condo with limited upside potential, it is easy to produce positive cash flow. While they may appear to have more cash flow on paper, the reality is that they will have higher maintenance costs, less appreciation, a weaker tenant profile (more damage, late or no rent) and increased vacancies and evictions.

Such properties will have limited potential for appreciation. When you look at all variables together, optimizing for a fixation on cash flow does not facilitate the greatest possible impact on long-term net worth.

Stronger properties with more upside potential cost more (increasing your denominator in your return on investment formula), and thus have higher carrying costs. However, they are more likely to be better long-term investments, with greater potential for appreciation, reduced maintenance costs, reduced vacancy and a stronger tenant profile.

I thus place less weight on positive cash flow and place a greater emphasis on the cumulative effect that the three variables – appreciation, cash flow and mortgage paydown – together have on net worth. This isn't to suggest that you should be breaking the bank monthly to carry your real estate properties. But it is to suggest that you need to look at the cumulative effect of the three variables and the properties with the greatest impact on your net worth, which may be close to a break-even cash flow monthly.

Mortgage Paydown

In the earlier example, the property had a $7,950 mortgage principal paydown per annum. My net worth increases by $7,950 per year simply by holding onto just this one property, all else remaining equal. And as luck would have it, the property was appreciating by $11,500 per annum.

My business generates cash flow and is the mechanism upon which I can pay for living expenses. My objective with real estate is to let it ride and to maximize the amount available during retirement, or, ideally, for the next generation.

A local author, having spent his life in real estate, similarly suggests the "point of investing in real estate is to create, grow and sustain wealth. Yet, real estate isn't a vehicle that will provide enough cash flow to live a lifestyle – at least not right away. It can be done, but I don't know many investors that have become full-time investors right away" (Davies, 2016, p. 4).

Julie Broad, real estate investor and author of *More Than Cashflow*, similarly notes that what "buy-and-hold lacks in cash today, it makes up for in cash tomorrow. Over time its value to you accelerates. The mortgage pays down faster and faster, and usually the appreciation grows year over year, on average. Ten years from now, that buy-and-hold property will be a beautiful bounty of cash if you need it" (Broad, 2013, p. 41).

Over time, your mortgage goes down and rental rates increase, thus easing pressures on cash flow and ultimately taking that break-even to a positive. And the combination of mortgage paydown and appreciation provides for significant equity in the property, delivering to you a substantial freedom of choice.

You can let it ride, continuing to build equity and enjoying increased cash flow or you can refinance and pull money out for further investments, whether that be another property or business acquisition. And banks love real estate. Having significant equity in a property on your balance sheet will make you a strong and stable entity in the eyes of lenders. Thus, real estate can be a critical piece to the success of financing your next business acquisition.

Should I Own my Personal Home?

Personal finance authors are split on this.

At the one extreme, commentators such as Robert Kiyosaki, author of *Rich Dad Poor Dad*, famously notes that a "house is a liability and if your house is your largest investment, you're in trouble", as houses do not always go up in value (Kiyosaki, 2017, p. 13). He further states, an "asset is something that puts money in my pocket whether I work or not. A liability is something that takes money out of my pocket. This is really all you need to know. If you want to be rich, simply spend your life buying or building assets. If you want to be poor or middle class, spend your life buying liabilities". (p 85).

Taking this argument one step further, most people tend to overbuy when it comes to an emotional decision, such as a house. When they overbuy, they overextend. When they overextend, much of their daily expenditures are allocated to interest payments, utilities, furnishings and constant upkeep and renovations. None of which adds to your net worth and, in fact, reduces your ability to consistently fund your three asset classes. Stretch "to buy your house and you'll inevitably stretch to buy your furnishings, your appliances and even your driveway decorations (i.e., your cars)" (Chilton, 2011, p. 73).

Overbuying a personal property can thus reduce your net worth, ongoing and irreparably. While this is true – that many people buy houses of a size and cost that is unnecessary (see later sections on consumerism) – owning your house is generally a great decision. Just be cognizant of what it is and is not providing. According to Stanley (2001) in *The Millionaire Mind*, nearly 97% of millionaires in their study are homeowners.

First, it may be the right decision for your family. And, as with our real estate discussion above, you are building mortgage paydown and appreciation.

With a personal house, you have 25 years of forced savings while you pay down your mortgage and then a lower cost of living beyond the mortgage paydown date.

And among the best contributor to your net worth is that the appreciation on your home is tax-free. Yes, if you own your home and it increases in value every year for 40 years, this is tax-free money in a world where almost every other form of earnings finds some heavy taxation at some point.

To realize the value of owning a home, you must have intentions of staying in the same home for an extended period of time. If you constantly move, you will be subject to mortgage insurance, realtor fees, mortgage payout penalties and market fluctuations – does that sound like a formula for building wealth?

However, it is best not to include your personal home in your net worth statement. Your net worth statement provides a picture of available resources and resources that have a singular purpose of compounding. Personal finance author Benz (2020, p. 21) notes, "our home is a place where we live, not an investment. If we were to move, it's likely that we would spend a like amount of money on housing, so housing-related assets just don't really figure into my thinking when I think about our assets".

In situations where you do not overextend and plan to occupy the house for a reasonable period of time, the choice of purchasing your personal home is a wise choice.

AN ENTREPRENEUR'S STRATEGY TO REAL ESTATE

My Strategy in Real Estate

I have explained real estate investing in a way for it to be a quasi-passive investment, to supplement your retirement, to appreciate and add to your net worth year after year.

My approach is to ensure that I have several single-family homes in areas that are most likely to appreciate. The properties are close to break-even cash flow (with a focus on appreciation foremost), are well taken care of and attract a strong tenant profile. Let's provide some details on such characteristics.

While residential real estate will never be completely hands-off, using the approach that I have suggested, investing in a handful of properties will provide enough equity to retire on and only require a part-time effort.

The time commitment lands somewhere between your business and that of your index funds. You can manage such investments without taking focus away from your business. And the good news is that as an entrepreneur, many skills overlap between business ownership and real estate investing, including negotiations, financing, managing people, advertising, insurance, legal and taxation.

I have chosen single-family homes for a number of reasons. In the residential space, the alternative would be condominiums, townhouses, duplexes or multiunit apartments. In the town that I invest in, I have trouble making the math work on most properties that have condo fees, which is relevant to condominiums and townhouses.

Once you factor in the condo fees, the properties tend to have negative cash flow. As an owner, you have no control over the amount of condo fees and most buildings do not have professional oversight. They are managed by a group of owners, who are without experience or training in this space. The condo board then hires a property management company to oversee the daily operations.

Mismanagement and inflation have contributed to condo fees exponentially increasing over the life of a building and have often led to surprise special assessments. Special assessments occur when there is an expense that has not been budgeted for and the reserve fund is not sufficient to cover the costs. The owners of the individual condo units (this would be you) are then expected to cover the cost of the unexpected expenses, the amount and timing of which you do not have any control over.

When people purchase a property, they make decisions based on the total carrying cost of the property. When condo fees are increased, the value of the property decreases as prospective buyers would require a reduced mortgage payment to offset the increase in condo fees. When condo fees are increased, the owner will see a reduced mortgage paydown and either a lower appreciation or, more likely, a position of devaluation of the property value.

Multiunit apartments can also be good investments, but require a different set of learnings as it is a different asset class with its own intricacies. They have the potential for a stronger cash flow given the operational synergies and a lower per-unit purchase price. However, their purchase price tends to start around one million dollars, making it a challenge for most individuals to enter as their first revenue property. When major repairs arise, they are significantly more costly and the asset can take longer to sell (less liquid) than a single-family home, which has a larger pool of prospective buyers.

Single-family properties have an easier learning curve, a more palatable entry price, are more liquid and attract a stronger tenant profile that is more likely to stay longer term. Even if you take a conservative approach and seek to have real estate as a base for retirement, you will require a base level of self-education on the topic.

Don Campbell (2009) notes 12 factors that affect real estate values in a particular location. Factors outside of your control that impact property values include: i) Changes in mortgage interest rates; ii) Increased average incomes in the area; iii) Increased net migration and demand for the target area; iv) Ripple effect from real estate values in surrounding areas; v) The local, regional and political climate; vi) Transportation expansion; and vii) Areas in transition. "As a sophisticated investor, you are looking for cities, towns or neighbourhoods that have as many of these factors in place as possible" (Campbell, 2009, p. 65).

You need to become familiar with these factors and how they affect your investment. The most important thing is understanding the specific areas you are targeting. How are these particular areas trending in terms of property values compared to other areas? Is there development in the area that is causing an increase in property values and desirability to live? What tenant profile will this area attract?

Given you only require a handful of properties to be able to retire, go ahead and take the time to research and make a decision that works best for you. Be very thoughtful and strategic about your purchases, as your buying decision on the property and area will have significant implications on your net worth; just a few good decisions provide a retirement base that most people must work a lifetime to achieve. Yet, buying the wrong property in the wrong area can cause significant reductions to your net worth.

Once you have acquired the properties, my approach is to let them ride. Similar to index funds, you will witness short-term fluctuations in property values as the economy moves through the various cycles. Entrepreneurs following a disciplined approach to an Impenetrable Financial Legacy look at real estate as a 30-, 40- or 50-year cycle, have the capacity not to panic, as they simply know that if they stick with it, the value of their properties will be worth more as they approach retirement.

Julia Broad notes: "What we've settled on for the bulk of our investment activities is what I would call a bread-and-butter approach. It's basic. It's easily repeatable. It's lower risk and it's less stressful. The returns are good but they aren't as large as some other strategies and they take time to materialize" (2013, p. 115).

As you purchase more properties over time, you will also see the benefits of the weighted cost average. And with a long enough time horizon, simply let the three pillars of cash flow, mortgage paydown and appreciation do the heavy lifting for you. As Bill Gates has been quoted as saying: "Most people overestimate what they can achieve in one year, but underestimate what they can achieve in ten years". This very much applies to the three variables of real estate.

Real Estate as a Business

You may frequently see other creative and more aggressive strategies suggested. If you wish to create a business out of real estate, you will be required to develop an expertise in more than one strategy, as buy-and-hold will not initially provide enough cash flow to pay a salary or to reinvest back into your real estate business for it to continue to grow at the required pace. Such strategies may include fix and flip, buy-renovate-rent-refinance, joint venture partnerships, rent to own, agreement for sale, aggressive lead generation systems, networking and property management systems.

For those who wish for it to be their primary business, such strategies must be employed. Such individuals will not only need to be more aggressive in asset accumulation, but also place a great emphasis on cash flow, in partial sacrifice to mortgage paydown and property appreciation. For these individuals, there will also be a greater pull on their time.

You do not need to take on this risk, nor are you required to pull your attention away from your business when you view real estate simply as one asset class in your portfolio. A simple buy-and-hold strategy, whereby you accumulate a select few single-family properties over an extended period of time, does not pull you off task or add risk to your portfolio and is enough to retire on with a long enough time horizon.

Eager speculators often view real estate as a get-rich-quick scheme and buy based on opportunity and not on a well-researched and developed strategy. Such individuals think more is better, and work toward a door count – how many properties can they accumulate – without thought to the purpose of such properties.

Campbell *et al*. note that "greed can manifest itself in the belief that the more real estate you accumulate, the better off you will be. This ignores the maxim that greater exposure to real estate does not guarantee success. In fact, consistently extending resources to accumulate real estate can have severe consequences, potentially making the financial burden too high to bear" (2011, p. 15).

"The truth is, without an effective strategy, more real estate will only cause more problems. Many investors believe random buying equals real estate success. There is misplaced faith in the market's ability to solve problems caused by lack of strategy" (Davies, 2016, p. 5).

Chapter Summary

In this chapter, I have demonstrated why estate is a great complementary asset class for entrepreneurs to own. While businesses tend to be a cash flow game, real estate is an equity game. With a part-time effort, your wealth receives the benefits of appreciation, mortgage paydown and cash flow.

As an entrepreneur, your time and energy are consumed by your business. Your real estate holdings must be set up in a way that strategically supports your overarching wealth goals, without competing for your time and energy. While residential real estate will never be completely hands-off, using the approach that I have suggested, investing in a handful of properties will provide enough equity to retire on and only require a part-time effort.

With only a small handful of residential properties, you can substantially add to your net worth, providing a further income stream that exists beyond you.

The goal is not to add risk to your portfolio, but to add a stable asset class that complements your business ownership, keeps pace with inflation, is tax-advantaged and consistently adds to your net worth year after year through the components of appreciation, mortgage paydown and cash flow.

The strategy detailed in this chapter is achievable, safe and extremely impactful on your net worth over the long term.

REFERENCES

Benz, Christine. "Christine Benz." In *How I Invest My Money: Finance Experts Reveal How They Save, Spend, and Invest*, edited by Joshua Brown and Brian Portnoy. Harriman House Ltd., 2020.

Broad, Julie. *More Than Cashflow: The Real Risks and Rewards of Profitable Real Estate Investing*. Stick Horse Publishing, 2013

Campbell, Don R. *Real Estate Investing in Canada: How to Create Wealth with the ACRE System*. John Wiley & Sons Canada Ltd., 2009.

Campbell, Don R., Kieran Trass and Greg Head. *Secrets of the Canadian Real Estate Cycle: An Investors Guide*. John Wiley & Sons Canada Ltd., 2011.

Chilton, David. *The Wealthy Barber Returns: Significantly Older and Marginally Wiser, David Chilton Offers His Unique Perspectives on the World of Money*. David Barr Chilton, 2011

Davies, Chris. *Apartment Buildings That Outperform: How to Build a Multi-Family Portfolio That Lasts*. Chris Davies, 2016.

Kiyosaki, Robert T. *Rich Dad Poor Dad: With Updates for Today's World*. Plata Publishing, 2017.

Stanley, Thomas J. *The Millionaire Mind*. Andrews McMeel Publishing, 2001.

Discipline to Execute Your Impenetrable Financial Legacy

Seven

If your retirement can be funded by any one of your three asset classes, then you have built up substantial wealth to leave a financial legacy. In this chapter, I outline how, with a focus on disciplines in your personal life, ultimately ensuring that your retirement goals can be funded by a singular asset class – your index funds. That should be substantial enough that you are not drawing down on it, but simply living off the income that it produces, with little interruption to the growth of your portfolio – your substantial wealth continues to grow, irrespective of life stages.

Let's make certain that you have the discipline to ensure there is no compromising on your public equity ownership, which guarantees your retirement, without exception. If we get this component right, you retire happy. Everything else becomes legacy.

To achieve this, mindset matters. Let's discuss how your personal philosophy is integral to achieving wealth.

There is an unlimited number of books on personal finances, financial planning and estate planning. I have read hundreds of these books. While valuable, such literature is tailored exclusively for the nine-to-fiver.

Some of this information is relevant, while much of it does not consider the massive impact your business ownership can

DOI: 10.4324/9781003724247-7

have on building wealth when armed with the exponential benefits of strategically utilizing the three asset classes.

Most of it focuses on retiring with enough. The information received is limiting your growth explosion. It does not recognize the potential we are all capable of when armed with knowledge of what could be and the discipline to achieve.

To put this system into practice, below I have included the most effective practices I have learned and placed them into a practical and achievable plan. After a lifetime of lessons – from successes and failures, and now to stability, I believe that I have provided you the best way to build an Impenetrable Financial Legacy.

These lessons form the foundational habits required to build intergenerational wealth from where you are now.

It Is Simple

Building wealth is simple. It isn't easy. But it's simple. Determine how large a portfolio you desire and reverse engineer – considering estimated rate of return and inflation – to calculate how much you must invest monthly to achieve that outcome. Then save and invest this amount each month and do not let anything take you off course.

Your plan will inevitably require you to spend less than you earn.

"If we study people who have gotten rich, we find that they are an average lot in all respects. It is evident that they do not get rich because they possess unique talents and abilities. They get rich because they happen to do things in a certain way" (Wattles, 2007, p. 8, originally published in 1910).

Why isn't everyone wealthy then? Because it is also easy to neglect the simple steps that it takes to become rich. They delay, make exceptions, excuses and before you know it, another year goes by. And with every year, it takes a significantly larger monthly investment to make up for the lost time.

Despite running out of money during retirement being among most people's biggest fears, financial neglect is common. Most people have seen family members, friends and neighbours suffer from issues that drain their finances, leading to diminished quality of life. Often this means being forced to work late into retirement when health does not permit, or having to rely on the goodwill of family, ultimately draining their chances of building wealth.

It is thus perplexing that while the fear is real, such fear is rarely translated into a disciplined approach of following an impenetrable financial strategy.

How Much Do You *Require?*

The famous quote from Bill Gates regarding personal achievement is quite relevant for investing as well: "People tend to overestimate what can be achieved in one year, but underestimate what can be achieved in ten years". Becoming a multi-millionaire sounds like a lot of money to the average person, but may not only be the amount you require, but also an amount that is very achievable.

Note that the goal of being a millionaire is no longer a prolific goal. Yet the term millionaire is still thrown around in the financial literature and by aspiring entrepreneurs as some laudable achievement. If you retire with one million dollars to your name, you might be above the poverty line, but will barely be hovering around the level of a living wage. And you will definitely not be building a legacy to pass on to the next generations.

While the term millionaire still has a nice ring to it, years of inflation have made the term obsolete. One million can no longer be your goal.

To calculate the size of an individual's required retirement fund, many personal finance authors draw on the four per cent rule. The rule states that if you withdraw four per cent of your total investment pool in your first year and stick with that same (inflation-adjusted) dollar amount each year, there is a safe probability that your retirement funds will last for 30 years.

For example, let's say you required $80,000 per year during your retirement. You would require a two-million-dollar retirement fund ($2,000,000 x 4% = $80,000, or $80,000 x 25 = $2,000,000).

Let's say that you determine that you require two million dollars in your retirement fund. If you start investing at age 25, you will only have to invest $570 per month for the 40 years between age 25 and age 65.[1]

The four per cent rule has been the general rule in the personal finance literature to determine the total asset value required at retirement. Note that it is simply a guideline and your situation will vary depending on the length of your retirement, the inflationary environment, the return on your assets, your health, whether your home is paid for and many other macroeconomic and personal variables.

There has also been a trend of people working into their retirement or returning to the workforce. Popular examples are starting a side hustle, consulting or taking up a different career, whether that be to supplement their pension or solely to maintain fulfilment.

Some personal finance authors have used this argument to suggest that you may not need to save as much as initially thought. The problem with this argument is that your health is never guaranteed. It is important to put yourself in a position where you can retire. This doesn't necessarily mean that you will retire, only that you have the option.

Chilton and others have suggested that individuals will require "between 60 and 70 percent of the average income of our last few working years to have an enjoyable retirement" (2011, p. 97). While you may have increased medical bills and longer vacations, a number of other expenditures will certainly be reduced, including child expenses, hopefully no mortgage and most of all, "there is no longer a need to set aside money for retirement" (2011, p. 98). If you have been setting aside 20% of your income for retirement, there is a 20% reduction in your monthly cash requirements from that alone.

It is important to note that only you can come up with your own retirement number. Only you know when you plan to retire, your health, the lifespan in your family history, whether you live a healthy lifestyle, what lifestyle you desire, what other assets and liabilities to consider and how much and which assets you wish to leave to your estate. And only you can own this number. Only you can be accountable for it.

Answer this now: How much do you need to retire? This is your number to own.

Of course, get professional support and second and third opinions on your wealth building plan, but it is you who must take ownership of the plan, not your accountant or financial planner.

While this is possible at any age, let's just say that the best time to invest was last year. If you missed that window, then start today (well, finish this book, take some notes, recommend it to a friend and then do it tomorrow, armed with a new plan!).

A Part of What I Earn Is Mine to Keep

Many entrepreneurs subconsciously default to paying themselves last, or, most typically, never. They pay their bills and use the rest to grow their business, all while ignoring their personal finances.

After calculating the amount of monthly investment required (required, not optional), some readers may feel that it is easily achievable, while others will struggle to consider how it would be possible to set aside such an amount.

When asked how much extra cash they have at the end of the month, the vast majority of people would have no idea. But the actual answer is most likely zero and a good portion of the population would have an ever-accumulating negative balance each month.

This is where pay yourself first comes into play.

The good news is that the personal financial literature is filled with book after book providing tips on how to allocate the required percentage of your income to investments.

As early as 1926, Clason published, "I found the road to wealth when I decided that a part of all I earned was mine to keep" (Clason, 1926, p. 17). Bach similarly notes, "Bottom line. No exaggeration. No hype. If you want to be rich, all you have to do is make a decision to do something that most people don't do. And that's to PAY YOURSELF FIRST" (2016, p. 62).

A long quote from *The Wealthy Barber*: "One of the most damaging misconceptions in personal finance is that saving for the future requires sacrifices today that lessen people's enjoyment of life. Surprisingly, it's quite the opposite! People who live within their means tend to be happier and less stressed. That's true not only for the obvious reason – they know their financial futures look bright – but also because they're not consumed with consumption. They're not in the emotionally and financially draining race to acquire the most stuff they possibly can. A race that, it should be noted, has no finish line and thus no winner" (Chilton, 2011, p. 117).

Once you have your investment level figured out, you can sleep at night knowing that your retirement is fully funded, you can continue to explore and grow in your best years and you can spend your remaining earnings as you wish, fully unincumbered and guilt-free.

While this is completely true, it cannot be denied that a high savings rate does not come with sacrifice.

The best explanation for this is in Sethi's book, *I Will Teach You to be Rich*. He notes, "What if you could make sure you were saving and investing enough money each month, and then use the rest of your money guilt-free for whatever you want? Well, you can – with some work. The only catch is that you have to plan where you want your money to go ahead of time" (Sethi, 2019, p. 128).

In a study of millionaires, Stanley and Danko find that wealth "is more often the result of a lifestyle of hard work, perseverance, planning, and, most of all, self-discipline" (2010, p. 2) and that being "frugal is the cornerstone of wealth-building" (p. 29).

It's rewarding and you will feel better every day knowing that you are on track. Take pride in what you are accomplishing. You will be happier and your relationships healthier. And there is a certain adrenaline when you contribute that little extra.

If you think living a life of discipline is hard, that setting aside for retirement is hard, wait until you get the bill for not doing so. It is a lot easier to save and provide for a purposeful life now than when you are retirement age, and your health does not allow you to fix the financial mistakes of your youth. Try being the old person with poor health and without a pension. Setting aside a few bucks every month seems a lot easier than living that lifestyle.

I have witnessed it all too often. People in their late 60s and 70s, pinching pennies, eating what they don't want to eat, driving what they don't want to drive, living where they don't want to live and going to work each day in physical pain, working at a place they don't want to work. It can all be traced back to a poor plan or a lack of discipline to execute that plan.

How Much Do You Desire?

The preceding section outlines what you must achieve to meet society's standards of retirement – to eat, have a roof over your head, have one vacation a year and leave a minimal estate behind. Is that really the definition of a purposeful life that you desire?

With your ambition and your business acumen, you are capable of so much more. Index fund investing for desire follows the same principles as investing for need. Except you enter it with an abundance mindset – your end number is higher, and you relentlessly execute to that number.

Your number is no longer based on survival or some societally derived valuation of having just enough. Rather, it is a number you achieve to fulfil your legacy and what that means to you specifically. Crank it up and achieve it.

You often hear people say, "You would never know they are wealthy." That is exactly the point. "Wealth is the nice cars not purchased. The diamonds not bought. The watches not worn, the clothes foregone and the first-class upgrade declined. Wealth is financial assets that haven't been converted into the stuff you see" (Housel, 2020, p. 98). "The world is filled with people who look modest but are actually wealthy and people who look rich who live at the razor's edge of insolvency. Keep this in mind when quickly judging others' success and setting your own goals" (p. 100).

Wealth and income are different. Income is what you earn; wealth is what you retain. You can become wealthy with good decisions while earning a modest income.

The happiest, wealthiest, most stable and content people I know do not appear affluent to the untrained eye. They live within their means and do not drive fancy cars or spend frivolously. They are content. They have a clear concept of what enough means to them. Many own blue-collar businesses and never lose sight of the hard work continually needed. They take pride in the continuous grind. They take pride in the financial cushions (the money not spent) that they have created for their family.

The good news is that this comes naturally for many business owners. As an entrepreneur, you will be used to tracking your income and expenses, keeping tabs on your personal balance sheet, and thinking long term. You will be aware of the true cost that routine expenditures have in perpetuity. You simply need to adopt this mindset in your personal life.

Keeping Up with the Joneses

Yet most people have a spending problem. They spend all their earnings and then some.

Most people have been programmed to define themselves by their material possessions – fancy houses, the latest technological gadgets, expensive clothes and new vehicles. It doesn't even need to be that extreme. Seemingly small habits can have an exponential impact on robbing your legacy.

Have more than one consumer package from Amazon arriving each month? You must change that obsession now.

It will be a lonely life if you choose to define yourself by your possessions. When we "express ourselves through material items, we lose our sense of who we are" (Jay, 2010, p. 285).

Consider the hangover almost everyone has in the weeks following holiday spending. Credit cards are maxed out and we buy more presents than originally intended. We all end up with things we don't need, that don't fit and that we will never use.

If you are normally able to set aside $2,000 a month to invest and you blow an extra $2,000 for the holidays, this means you worked a full month (delayed your financial freedom and retirement by a full month, multiplied by your whole career) to buy items that may never be used. "Inflatable reindeer and piles of presents do not make a joyous holiday; gathering with our loved ones does" (Jay, 2010, p. 15).

Wouldn't it be great if your children learned that the holidays were about family and friends and not about consumerism? And if they were learning by example how to respect money? How to carry on the financial legacy that you are creating. Would they appreciate – albeit partially in retrospect – help with tuition in lieu of that additional tenth gift that they will outgrow within months?

After a period of non-routine and high spending, you will be motivated for a change in spending patterns. Try a month of essentials only. This will not only be a great month for your savings and investment, but, more importantly, it will help to reset spending habits.

"The fact of the matter is, once we've covered our basic needs, our happiness has very little to do with the amount of stuff we own. Beyond this point, the marginal utility (or satisfaction) derived from consuming additional goods diminishes rapidly" (Jay 2010, pp. 15–16).

You will inevitably have clutter and busyness in your business. It will consume your energy. So, it is important to simplify and declutter your personal life. Don't let consumerism occupy your mind 24/7. And further consider how much time you spend running errands, shopping online, researching products that you will use for a couple of months and then become out of fashion.

Cutting that streaming service subscription isn't just about the $14 a month saved; it is about the time that you waste each day that could be spent building relationships, exercising or learning.

Change your habits now. It gets harder to change course on the materialistic urge the longer it goes on.

Another valuable way to save is to set aside any irregular surprise money – or a portion thereof – into your investment account. If you have an unexpected tax return, inheritance, your vacation costs less than you thought, cash back from the bottle depot, negotiated a reduced price on a purchase, sell an item you no longer require, or decide to cancel that streaming service ... get excited about putting this amount into your investment account. After a while, you will get excited when you find savings, as it means you are one step closer to financial freedom.

Rather than spending on visible consumer goods, wealth accumulation is invisible. It is your reinvestment into your business (marketing, acquisitions, capital replacement), cash automated to tax-advantaged accounts and funds allocated to real estate down payments. The size of each of these buckets compounds over time, until eventually you are able to live off the cash that they produce. When doing this right, it comes much quicker than you think.

Housel defines savings as "the gap between your ego and your income" (Housel, 2020, p. 106). It is thus how much you save, consistently, month after month, that defines your wealth.

Wealth is also a mindset of not coveting what your neighbour has for possessions. One of the all-time greatest investors, Charlie Munger, is famous for saying that "Envy is the only sin that you can't have fun doing". And it is so true. Envy, jealousy and resentment – each driving consumerism behaviours – only wreak havoc on your mental state.

Helpful tips to accelerate your investment strategy include:

- Determine your desired wealth future and then arrange your life to achieve this. No exceptions, no excuses;
- Determine that health, relationships and financial freedom derive happiness. Consumer goods are an addiction with only short-term adrenaline;
- Hit your monthly investment goals, without excuse, month over month, year after year;
- Pay yourself first. And then spend what is left over;
- Assign any surprise money (e.g. returned items, inheritances, government forgiveness programmes, etc.) directly to your investment account.

If you do these things, you are well on your way to building an Impenetrable Financial Legacy.

CONSUMERISM KILLS LEGACY

Consumerism is among the top enemies in your journey towards achieving financial independence. While we have already introduced personal finances, consumerism deserves its own section within this topic.

It adds stress to your life, crushes your chance of a peaceful retirement and goes as far as breaking up marriages. Even those who claim to be good with money should take a serious self-reflection when reading this section.

Becoming wealthy requires a change in mindset. "Becoming financially independent as the result of developing million-dollar habits is a great goal, but it is not the most important thing. It is the person you must become, in terms of courage, character, thoughtfulness, and persistence, that is most important. As a result of becoming financially successful over a long period of time, you will feel truly happy and satisfied with yourself, and with every other part of your life" (Tracy, 2017, p. 81).

As with knowing your personal balance sheet, it is also important to understand your personal income statement – what are the inflows and outflows of your cash every month? I am not suggesting living by a strict budget, meticulously tracking every expense for the rest of your life. But it is important to understand your baseline when starting the process of becoming wealthy.

Start with a blank sheet and identify a list of what is important to you in your life. If you had limited funds, as we all do, what areas are important to you to continue with your desired lifestyle? What aspects of your life do you not wish to compromise on?

For example, books, education, continuous learning or gifts on special occasions for my nieces top my list, while dining out and driving fancy cars do not. But only you can determine what is important to you. Your list could look the opposite to mine and that is perfectly fine.

Next, construct a snapshot of the past three months. Identify every expense that occurred over this period, then sort them into themes. Everyone will have themes of housing, groceries, transportation, but other themes may be unique to your spending patterns, such as coffees, clothing, events, dining out, hobbies, etc.

How do these themes compare to what you said was important to you? If you did not identify coffee or dining out as important to you, yet they occupy a significant expense each month, consider mercilessly cutting this expense.

If your daily coffee is seven dollars and you buy one on your way to work each weekday, you are spending approximately $146 per month. That money, invested at eight percent over a 40-year working career, is approximately $510,000 at retirement. Is your morning coffee worth over half a million dollars to you? Likely not. Continue this exercise for every expense category on your list.

Delaying expenses is also a great tactic for reduced spending. If you want something, put it on your list or leave it in your online shopping cart for a few weeks. More often than not, as time passes, the excitement wears off and you decide not to bother with the purchase.

Areas that you identified as important to you, continue spending as you wish. I am not suggesting you sacrifice things that are important to you. Following this exercise, most people can identify enough with the misalignment between unimportant to them and areas of expenditure, making very few alterations to their life to get on a track of financial independence.

Repeat this exercise every year to make sure that you stay on track.

The early years of wealth building is when such focus on your habits is the most important. Minor changes to daily habits in your expenditures are notable in ruthlessly building your asset base and are the foundation on which all future gains are accumulated.

But once you are earning bigger money, small items such as coffees and dining out start to form a negligible amount relative to your monthly contributions, so they will not derail your progress. However, you will notice that once you have built in strong financial habits and have high self-worth, you will no longer crave such consumerism.

Do the math unique to your personal situation.

Consumer Debt

Those who can sustain a high net worth for the long run also never take on consumer debt. Note that I didn't say *rarely*; I said *never*. Consumer debt includes any personal credit accounts used for personal or household purchases, including automotive loans, loans for holiday trailers or recreational vehicles, credit card debt or credit for any other personal items, such as furniture or electronics. For purposes of this section, I am not including mortgages or student loans, which can play a purpose in wealth creation.

Consumer debt works directly against wealth accumulation, as any resources that would otherwise be working toward building your net worth are reallocated towards personal loans. Such loans usually carry high interest rates.

Sometimes consumer goods are offered at a low interest rate to encourage overspending (e.g. zero percent interest for the first year). When this occurs, the price is inflated to make up for the lost time value of money for the manufacturer selling the goods. Overindulgence costs you lost wealth one way or another.

The Car that Cost $2.8 Million

The combination of high interest rates and the short nature of term loans makes such debt a strain on your monthly cash available for investing.

Vehicles depreciate. Their short-term and high-interest-rate nature are detrimental to your debt service ratios, making it difficult to qualify for loans that will help build your wealth – like a mortgage or a business acquisition.

It is for these reasons that Stanley and Danko found that "fewer than 25 percent of America's millionaires are driving the current year's model" (2010, p. 87). And quite interestingly, their survey of millionaires also noted that the value of their most expensive vehicle "equates to less than 1 percent" of their net worth, whereas "typical motor vehicle buyers spend the equivalent of at least 30 percent of their net worth for such purchases" (2010, p. 114).

To demonstrate the perils of consumer debt, let's say you finance a new Honda Civic (a seemingly sensible and economical vehicle) with a $40,000 loan over five years at eight percent interest. The payments are roughly $800 per month. Over the five years, you will have paid $48,500 in payments for that vehicle. If you plan to always own a similar vehicle on similar terms, this $800 would be a perpetual spend.

Five years later, the car would be worth about $22,000 dollars. So you have spent over $8,000 in interest payments and lost $18,000 in depreciation.

Alternatively, if you were to pay cash for a much lower amount and rerouted this same $800 towards an index fund that returned eight per cent between the ages of 25 and 65, you would have an extra $2.8 million at retirement (or using 11%, not counting for inflation, would be $6.9 million).

Do this calculation for your own vehicle. If you are serious about building wealth, you may have to make serious adjustments. This finding is a good gut check on the priorities of the wealthy and the disciplined habits we need to face to achieve wealth.

Yes, you need a reliable vehicle, especially when transporting kids in a Canadian winter. But this doesn't mean that you require a *new* vehicle. Take the time to do some research and search for condition and mileage as opposed to year. Condition and mileage relate to value, vehicle age correlates to ego, debt and a lack of savings.

Let some other broke sucker buy the vehicle new, make the expensive interest payments in lieu of investing and then buy it from them just a few years later for half the price.

How much of your net worth does this depreciating asset constitute? If it is more than about 3–5%, you have some work to do, both on your expenditure (numerator) and on your wealth accumulation (denominator). If your vehicle is pushing upward of 10% of your net worth, you require some serious reflection on whether that aligns with the exercise on priorities above.

Note that I am speaking in percentages. Once you have made significant strides to becoming wealthy, a vehicle that is a mere one per cent of your net worth could be a brand new top-of-the-line auto. You have earned the right to indulge. And the expense is inconsequential to your continued trajectory. But until then, don't let consumerism and ego knock you off course.

Once I got serious about the topics in this book, my vehicle went from being about 3.5% to being well under 1% in a period of three years by altering both variables.

With a cursory observation, you will identify many humble people in your life driving modest vehicles. And broke people driving new ones. One of my friends is a master at this, still driving a 1996 truck that he bought about 20 years ago. He is a self-made multi-millionaire.

On top of that, the vehicle that he drives is owned by his company. Not only is it fully paid for, with no monthly payments, but every dollar spent on transportation – tires, maintenance, fuel, insurance, registration – is a tax deduction inside his company.

There is never a good reason for personal debt other than a mortgage.

I use vehicles as an example, because they have the greatest swing and provide for a very tangible example, but you can follow the same logic for rent, clothes, and any other routine expenditures that adults tend to overindulge on, yet that are more likely to add financial stress to our lives than they are to add happiness.

SERIOUS MONEY IS LONG-TERM MONEY

Farmers give the best advice because they think in 100-year cycles. They have long memories of their businesses with stories and mentorship passed down from generations past. They are disciplined not to risk the long-term endurance of their business for short-term gains, as they often plan to pass on their business to future generations.

My friend Tim is a multigenerational farmer and owner of numerous businesses. Discussing entrepreneurship on our way to watch a hockey game, he made a comment that stuck with me: "This is not a business to panic in". The subtext of this was to think long-term and not to make short-term decisions out of panic or fear. Commodity prices fluctuate but will return to equilibrium at some point.

My colleague Brad also operates a multigenerational farm that has grown steadily under his leadership. His advice: "Never work backwards". If you are always moving forwards, incremental gains, year after year, will get you to where you want to go.

"The fact is that serious money is long-term money. Most wealthy people organize their financial lives in such a way that their net worth increases about 8 to 10 precent per year on the amount of money they have working. They do not look for get-rich-quick schemes or easy money. They are patient, persistent, and farsighted. They discipline themselves to save and accumulate money over many years. They do not speculate, take risks, or look for fast ways to make money quickly and easily. Because of these habitual ways of thinking about their money each year their wealth grows. Eventually, they pass the million-dollar mark and usually keep on going" (Tracy, 2017, p. 70).

Mitigating Risk (Never Work Backwards)

In a speech that I was fortunate to attend, Greg Abel, the successor of Warren Buffett, commented on Buffett's philosophy. He noted that Buffett, in focusing on the long-term, has a mind for anticipating risk. Referring to conversations with Buffett when examining the acquisition of a company, Abel noted: "What are the risks. I have never heard him talk about growth. How do we understand the problems? How do we address them as an organization?"

Invert your thinking. Consider all the things that could bring your business down. Consumer trends, lawsuits, customer attrition, slow growth, staff morale, organizational reputation, excessive debt. Track them and react to them. Determine what is important and ensure management reports on it.

When explaining this inversion concept, both Munger and Buffett often comment: "All I want to know is where I'll die so I'll never go there".

In a revised version of the *Intelligent Investor*, Zweig notes that "the intelligent investor must focus not just on getting the analysis right. You must also ensure against loss if your analysis turns out to be wrong – as even the best analyses will be at least some of the time. The probability of making at least one mistake at some point in your investing lifetime is virtually 100%, and those odds are entirely out of your control. However, you do have control over the consequences of being wrong" (Zweig in Graham, 2003, p. 530).

In reference to the dot-com bubble, Zweig further suggests: "Certain that they knew the probabilities of being right, they did nothing to protect themselves against the consequences of being wrong. Simply by keeping your holdings permanently diversified, and refusing to fling money at Mr. Market's latest, craziest fashions, you can ensure that the consequences of your mistakes will never be catastrophic" (Zweig in Graham, 2003, p. 530).

Losing money that you have is not only financially devastating but emotionally as well. It is demoralizing.

Some of the best advice I have had is to never work backwards. And to not risk what you have already accumulated.

Often, after working through the above formula and determining a path that will achieve wealth, albeit slowly and safely, people then become impatient and want to expedite the process.

Expediting their timeline usually requires cashing out on a tried and true asset and reallocating the proceeds towards "an investment" that promises an accelerated return. However, the accelerated return inevitably comes with higher risk. When done on a whim, it is often in a space unfamiliar to you – outside of your circle of competence – whereby you have less ability to properly research and understand and with factors further removed from your control.

"Like all of life's rich emotional experiences, the full flavor of losing important money cannot be conveyed by literature. Art cannot convey to an inexperienced girl what it is truly like to be a wife and mother. There are certain things that cannot be adequately explained to a virgin either by words or pictures. Nor can any description that I might offer here even approximate what it feels like to lose a real chunk of money that you used to own" (Schwed, 1940, p. 54).

I wish I had understood the concepts of incremental gains, risk mitigation, diversification, dollar cost averaging and liquidity earlier in my entrepreneurial journey. It would have saved much pain and reduced the sleepless nights, stressing over debt obligations.

As I noted in *Faster Safer Wealthier*, "If I could tell my 24-year-old self one thing about wealth, I would say: you do not have to take significant risks in order to become wealthy, as substantial wealth can be accumulated through a structured process of incremental gains. You do not have to risk current wealth in order to accumulate further wealth" (Bott, 2021, p. 189). Rather, "A steady path of incremental gains is rarely risky and focuses on wealth retention in parallel to wealth accumulation" (Bott, 2021, p. 190).

Most successful wealth holders became that way over time. They protected themselves from working backwards. Never lose money. At the very least, never lose big money.

NOTE

1 Sethi (2019) notes the average return of the stock market over the 20th century to be 11%. The Bank of Canada states an average inflation rate of just under 3% over the past 100 years. Note that most assumptions throughout this book thus use an 11% stock market return and 3% inflation. An inflation adjusted return of approximately 8% thus seems like a reasonable estimation for calculating stock market returns.

REFERENCES

Bach, David. *The Automatic Millionaire: A Powerful One-Step Plan to Live and Finish Rich*. Penguin Random House, 2016.

Bott, Gregory. *Faster Safer Wealthier: Skip the Start-up and Buy a Stable Business to Build Intergenerational Wealth*. Abja Inc., 2021.

Chilton, David. *The Wealthy Barber Returns: Significantly Older and Marginally Wiser, David Chilton Offers His Unique Perspectives on the World of Money*. David Barr Chilton, 2011.

Clason, George S. *The Richest Man in Babylon*. Reprinted. Penguin Random House, 2019.

Housal, Morgan.. *The Psychology of Money: Timeless Lessons on Wealth, Greed, and Happiness*.Harriman House Ltd., 2020.

Jay, Francine. *The Joy of Less, A Minimalist Living Guide: How to Declutter, Organize, and Simplify Your Life*. Anja Press, 2010.

Schwed Jr, Fred. *Where are the Customers' Yachts?: or a Good Hard Look at Wall Street*. John Wiley & Sons Inc., 1940.

Sethi, Ramit. *I Will Teach You to be Rich: No Guilt. No Excuses. No BS. Just a 6-Week Program That Works*. Second Edition. Workman Publishing Co., 2019.

Stanley, Thomas J. and William D. Danko. *The Millionaire Next Door: The Surprising Secrets of America's Wealthy*. Taylor Trade Publishing, 2010.

Tracy, Brian. *Million Dollar Habits: Proven Power Practices to Double & Triple Your Income*. Entrepreneur Press, 2017.

Wattles, Wallace D. *The Science of Getting Rich: Attracting Financial Success Through Creative Thought*. Reprinted. Destiny Books, 2007.

Zweig, Jason. "Commentary on Chapter 20." In *The Intelligent Investor: A Book of Practical Council, Revised Edition*. HarperCollins Publishers Inc., 2003.

Bonus Chapters

Eight

CASH AND LIQUIDITY

When building and protecting wealth, it is important to have an understanding of liquidity and of the consequences of either too little (places wealth retention at risk) or too much (reduces the rate of wealth building) liquidity.

Liquidity is the ability to convert a particular asset into cash without losing value in the process. As there is often a trade-off between liquidity and return, it is important to find the right balance of liquidity (e.g., cash on hand) while ensuring that the vast majority of your assets are out there working for you.

So far, the assets you have been accumulating from reading this book have varied in their level of liquidity. Real estate, for example, is relatively illiquid. If you decide to sell, it may take time to provide concessions to the tenants, it may sit on the market for months and then take another month for the deal to close. If a deal falls through, you have to start the process all over. And when you do sell, you lose significant value to realtor fees, mortgage payout penalties and other closing costs. Appreciation may be subject to capital gains tax.

Small businesses can take a long time to sell, if you can sell them at all, and are subject to similar issues with long timelines, deals that fall through, significant closing costs and possible capital gains taxation.

DOI: 10.4324/9781003724247-8

Index funds inside an RRSP can be sold but are subject to heavy taxation. You may also be selling during a downturn in the market. And, most detrimentally, you are reducing your base for future compounded returns between now and retirement.

TFSAs are more liquid than RRSPs. You can take money out and regain that contribution room the following year. There are no tax implications from the withdrawal. If you replace it in a timely manner, it has fewer implications than when drawing down on other assets.

However, I do not recommend touching your retirement fund under any circumstances until you have built it up to a level where you are guaranteed financial independence. Once you start tampering with your automated wealth-building system, it is a slippery slope.

If you are constantly in a cash crunch – high net worth or not – you are forced to make decisions that are detrimental to long-term wealth building to meet short-term obligations.

I love liquidity. I love the freedom that comes with liquidity. Having access to cash or cash equivalents means you can act quickly on deals. If you have a delay in getting paid by a customer, require a down payment on a piece of equipment, want to complete a small acquisition, it's no problem. With a liquid position, you can also take advantage of bear markets and buy more stocks when the market is down.

There are many uncertainties in life: Your business might require a capital injection, your rental property might require an unexpected major repair or you might experience the death of a business partner. Always be prepared for a downturn in the economy, an increase in interest rates chewing up your cash, or a shift in consumer trends slowing down your sales. Only with a margin of safety – liquidity – can you ride these out.

Save cash in the good times because the tough times are inevitable. The challenge most people face is a level of greed in the good times, a feeling that the boom in the economy will never end, so they invest their last dollar, or worse yet, take on crazy debt loads.

"When cash is plentiful, good decisions are more difficult. You need to find balance between hoarding it for safety and employing it to grow and seize opportunities" (Pritchett, 2006, p. 57).

The only way for a business to die is for it to run out of cash. There are hundreds of ways for a business to run out of cash, many of which are only obvious in hindsight.

When you have liquidity, you are not at the mercy of the bank, which can take weeks and multiple rounds of documentation to get approved for a loan. You do not have to withdraw your RRSPs and pay a substantial tax liability.

You have the upper hand against competing bids when you can pay cash for a deal while the next person's offer is subject to financing, which means the seller would have to wait weeks or months to receive their funds. Your offer is much more attractive and you will have more bargaining power on the terms.

While it is important to have some level of liquidity – on the upper level, the ability to move on deals, and on the lower end, at least a margin of safety – having too much liquidity leads to an opportunity cost, as there tends to be a correlation between committing your capital over the long term and the opportunity for an increased return. Real estate is a long game, index funds should be a long game and your business is definitely a long game.

Cash is your lowest risk asset – a short-term asset – which means it also provides for the lowest potential return.

When your cash isn't invested in these assets – out there working for you – it is not providing for a return. You can compensate for this by investing in short-term, guaranteed investment certificates or placing your money in high-interest savings accounts. But such investments tend not to outpace inflation, meaning if you are sitting on too much cash, you are actually working backwards.

Find a balance that works for you.

Lines of Credit

One way to ensure liquidity is to have a line of credit. This way, you can keep less cash on hand and deploy your cash and other assets based on your desired allocation, knowing that your line of credit allows you to retain liquidity and act quickly when needed. It provides for flexibility and peace of mind.

A line of credit is a credit account whereby you can draw down as you desire, pay it back and draw down on it again. Payments for interest accumulated on the balance are due each month, but you are not required to pay down the principal amount on any particular schedule. Lines of credit are commonly advanced by banks for companies that operate on a cyclical billing cycle, where they incur a cost of goods expense up front and a delay in being paid for the matching revenue.

Farms are probably the best example: A farmer has extensive expenses in preparation for seeding their crops in the spring, but does not receive any revenue until after their harvest, which can be six or more months later. The farmer can draw down on the principal amount, pay interest on the balance for the period and then pay it down as revenue comes in months later. Then the next year, the loan is still active and can be drawn down again as they enter another business cycle. Having continued access to it provides the predictability of liquidity.

You are also able to obtain a line of credit in your personal name, although there are limitations to the amount you can receive unsecured from an individual bank. After that limit, they seek security, such as your personal home.

If you know you have discipline with money and can separate your businesses' needs from your personal indulgences, having access to multiple and large lines of credit can be a great thing. You will want to aim for a significant enough amount, whereby when you do use them, you are able to stay within a low utilization ratio, to build your credit rating and not hinder your credit score.

In Berkshire Hathaway's 1980 letter to shareholders, Warren Buffett comments: "The most attractive opportunities may present themselves at a time when credit is extremely expensive – or even unavailable. At such a time we want to have plenty of financial firepower" (1980, p. 15).

Take lines of credit when your income and balance sheet look attractive to banks – so that you have them when you do need them but wouldn't otherwise qualify for them. A line of credit can be the ultimate tool in eliminating the required trade-off between liquidity and return. Having cash on hand means that it is not out there working for you.

This makes a line of credit a perfect solution – your cash can be out there making a return, while your line of credit is providing that safety net. Knowing that you have access to a flexible loan on demand reduces the amount of cash you need to have on hand. You can simply draw down on your line of credit as necessary.

However, it can also be quite dangerous if you are not prudent in your plan to pay down the principal on a structured schedule or prior to the next business cycle. David Chilton, author of *The Wealthy Barber*, suggests that "lines of credit are like giant credit cards but with much lower interest rates and no travel points. And like their plastic cousins, LOCs allow us to mindlessly give in to temptation and live beyond our means. [...] People have gone wild with these things over the last two decades. Can't afford something? No worries, just 'throw it on the line of credit'" (2011, p. 48).

I do not feel that those warnings apply to the readers of this book. If you use them wisely, create a psychological firewall to separate them from consumer expenditures and have a structured plan to pay down any amounts used, they can be a great tool for those looking to build wealth. It is when people use them for consumer purchases, such as a vehicle purchase, a boat, a wedding, a kitchen renovation or simply lifestyle creep, that they get themselves into trouble.

PROTECT YOUR CREDIT RATING

It is almost inevitable that business owners will seek credit at some point in their journey and a residential mortgage will be necessary to execute your Impenetrable Financial Legacy as laid out in this book. It is important to understand and monitor your credit score, so that credit is available to you on the best possible terms.

Credit bureaus collect information about your credit history and compile this information into a credit report. Lenders, such as banks, access this information about you when you apply for a loan. The information displayed on your credit report includes identifying information (e.g., your name, address history, social insurance number, date of birth and employment history), a list of your credit accounts (type of account, date it was opened, your credit limit on each account, account balance and payment history), enquiry information (what companies have you sought to acquire credit from) and public court records regarding information such as collections or bankruptcy.

There are two main credit bureaus in Canada – Equifax and TransUnion – and each will have a file on you if you have had any type of loan with financial institutions in the past. It is extremely important for entrepreneurs to maintain a strong credit score. When you seek a loan either for business (e.g. fixed loans for equipment, lines of credit) or personal use (mortgage, lines of credit), your credit report and credit score are accessed by lenders and used to help evaluate your risk level – the probability of you being able to repay your loan based on your track record.

When a prospective lender pulls your credit report, they can see your credit score, verify outstanding balances on existing loans and review your payment history on existing and past loans.

If you have a strong history of using debt responsibly, you will be perceived as a lower risk candidate to lend money to, thus not only increasing your odds of a loan approval but also receiving more favourable loan terms, such as a lower interest rate or increased amortization.

As an entrepreneur, access to capital is extremely important. In the past two months alone, I have added a residential mortgage, increased our lines of credit on two businesses and received a fixed-term business loan for a new business.

The lending criteria for the residential mortgage was based on my personal ability to service the debt along with my credit rating. The business loan was based on the business's ability to service the debt, along with my personal credit score. Needless to say, for an entrepreneur, access to capital is important – whether that be for buying or expanding a business or adding to your real estate portfolio.

How do you ensure that you maintain a strong credit report and thus a high credit score?

- Average age of accounts: The average age of accounts is a factor in calculating your credit score. To build up a credit score, you must have a credit history. The longer you have each credit account, the better. Thus, once you have obtained a loan, especially revolving loans like a line of credit or a credit card, it is best to leave them open and not close your account. You can use some logic as to which loans to keep open, but do not continually open and close loans. If you are seeking additional credit, it is best to increase the value of existing loans rather than to seek new loans;
- Credit utilization rate: It is important to be cognizant of your credit utilization rate. It is best to keep your credit utilization rate low, meaning to not always use the full amount of credit available. You are demonstrating responsible use of a line of credit, for example, if you generally are only using 30% or less of your total available credit. Increasing your available limit on your line of credit or credit card is one way of maintaining a low credit utilization rate. Keep your limit high but your balance low;
- The number of recent credit applications: Try not to apply for multiple new credit accounts in a short period of

time. This is a signal that you are in a poor financial position and are seeking funds urgently. Multiple enquiries are also a signal that each enquiry is a result of being rejected in the previous enquiry. Even if you are successful in obtaining credit, the new credit account will decrease the average age of your accounts, thus also affecting your credit score;

- Review your report often: When trying to affect your credit score, it is important to have a baseline understanding of what is contained in your credit report. You should review your report to see which of your lenders are reporting to the agencies, what your limits are, what your payment history is and how long each credit account been open. Review it often. You are able to access your report infrequently for free. But it is best to increase the frequency with which you review your report. By doing so, you can identify any errors or fraudulent activity or identity theft. It is also important to view your report before applying for credit to ensure your credit application and balance sheet are consistent with what is being reported on your credit report;
- Payment history: A repetitive history of meeting your payment obligations will build your score over time. The alternative, missing payments, will bring down your credit score. I have most of my bills, including my credit card, automatically withdrawn from my account, making it impossible to make a payment late.

It seems like everyone wants to pull your credit report these days for frivolous reasons, including when opening a utility account, seeking small amounts of credit from vendors or applying for business loans. Say no and find a different pathway to the services that you require. When I was setting up temporary utilities for our latest rental property, the electricity company required a credit check in order to set up the account. I said no and moved on to the next company, which didn't require a credit check. The fuel suppler where one of my companies purchases petroleum from wanted a credit check to increase my credit limit. I said no and went to the next company and had no issues.

Do not apply for additional credit cards or small loans that will not add value to you or your business. Protect your credit rating by being extremely frugal with those who want to pull your credit report for frivolous reasons.

Sethi (2019) notes that "establishing good credit is the first step in building an infrastructure for getting rich. Think about it: Our largest purchases are almost always made on credit, and people with good credit save tens of thousands of dollars on these purchases. Credit has a far greater impact on your finances than saving a few dollars a day on a cup of coffee" (p. 30).

REFERENCES

Buffett, Warren. *Berkshire Hathaway's 1980 Letter to Shareholders*. Berkshire Hathaway, 1980.

Chilton, David. *The Wealthy Barber Returns: Significantly Older and Marginally Wiser, David Chilton Offers His Unique Perspectives on the World of Money*. David Barr Chilton, 2011.

Sethi, Ramit. *I Will Teach You to be Rich: No Guilt. No Excuses. No BS. Just a 6-Week Program That Works*. Second Edition. Workman Publishing Co., 2019.

Putting It All Together

Nine

YOUR IMPENETRABLE FINANCIAL LEGACY

At the beginning of the book, you were asked if your business were to fail or flounder, would your personal finances be affected? After following the steps in this book, your response now will be a resounding "no".

You will have selected a profitable business that endures and will have taken further steps to ensure its endurance continues. You will have a stable portfolio of index funds that have accumulated to a size whereby, viewed in isolation, you would be able to live a fruitful and happy retirement. Your properties continue to appreciate, mortgages decrease daily and now provide a monthly cash return.

Planning this way gives you options. If you want to hand down your properties or business to the next generation, you can live off your stock portfolio; if one asset class is down at the time of retirement, draw down on a portion of a different one; if one is highly taxed, you have others that do not count as income upon accessing them.

Once you implement your personalized financial plan and asset allocation, based on the principles outlined in this book, your net worth simply increases each year, year after year.

It is quite surprising and a great feeling. It might feel like you are still in the daily grind, but when you update your net

DOI: 10.4324/9781003724247-9

worth template, it is such a great feeling to see all the individual factors making a significant cumulative effect.

When you stick to the fundamentals, a typical year will look as follows:

Your Business

After significant reflection, Jennifer chose to sell off what was left of her original business. During this reflection, she learned what it means to be an enduring business. This informed her search criteria and, after two years of searching for a business, she landed one that has much better fundamentals and will continue to be around for the long haul.

And with an understanding of risk mitigation, she works every day on the big picture of the business. What could create risk for the business and how can she mitigate against this, ultimately protecting the business from external and internal disruption?

She spends her mornings reading, learning and focusing on the things that are the most impactful to her business and to her future. She still works hard every day. But her focus has shifted towards thought and away from the daily minutiae that she was once consumed with. This allows her businesses to flourish. Her guidance to her business partners and her coaching to her business managers are better informed. Her decisions are impactful.

Thinking not just like an entrepreneur, but as an investor, she is very methodical about her capital allocation and every dollar earned is preallocated to its highest and best use. She will now arrive at a planned destination, not an unplanned destination.

Just like Jennifer's, your business will have steady growth. This growth allows for economies of scale, whereby each additional revenue provides for a slightly higher percentage of net revenue. The additional earnings increase your net worth as the business is now worth more if you were to sell it. Some of the additional earnings will stay in your business to fund the required capital to service new demand or to fund growth through acquisitions.

Some of the revenue will go towards increased disbursements to the owner(s). When the owner does not allow for lifestyle creep and continues to live on the amount of their previous paycheck, the additional disbursements are allocated towards a rebalancing of your asset allocation – to index funds, property down payments, additional businesses or cash and other liquid reserves.

Once you have achieved financial independence, you may choose to allow for an increased lifestyle. That is your choice. Just don't do it too prematurely.

Although you have taken steps to ensure that your business endures, you never place your life and your heir's future in the hands of a single business, regardless of how sure you are of its future returns. You have substantial and sustainable assets across the three asset classes.

Your Real Estate

The cash earned from your real estate holdings may be insignificant and any cash earned will most likely be required to stay in the real estate bank account to fund future repairs. However, over a long enough runway, you will be making significant gains on your mortgage principal paydown and see appreciation of your individual properties and thus of your portfolio.

This appreciation increases your net worth and provides a potential platform to refinance and purchase additional properties. My favourite characteristic of real estate holdings is mortgage paydown. Your net worth increases month after month, year after year, simply by paying your mortgage payments. You just need the discipline and perseverance to hold on for the ride.

The net worth advantages of residential real estate are based on three pillars: appreciation, cash flow and mortgage paydown. With a long enough time horizon, simply let the three do the heavy lifting for you.

With your properties appreciating and your mortgages decreasing, you have built substantial wealth in real estate. You have more wealth in just this one asset class than the total your peers have accumulated in their lifetime.

You could cash out, but you don't have to. Your index funds alone are enough to live off. So you hold on for the ride, teaching your kids the same financial principles that have propelled the Impenetrable Financial Legacy that you have created for them. The portfolio continues to grow under their watch.

Index Funds

Since your time is already overextended within your business, you will not be successful if the other aspects of your financial life require the same degree of time commitments. You would simply end up overcommitted and doing a poor job across all asset classes, ultimately leading to poor returns, negating your initial purpose for wealth building.

Index funds are among the simplest, yet most effective, means of investment strategy. In this book, I have demonstrated their effectiveness when utilized in conjunction with steadfast discipline and dollar cost averaging.

Stick with it, recognizing that lows in the market are not times to panic, but present a purchasing opportunity whereby the asset you seek has been placed on sale.

To both grow and preserve your wealth, you must maximize your tax advantaged accounts first – namely your RRSP and TFSA accounts – before then shifting towards non-tax advantaged accounts.

While your index funds may be overshadowed by the success of your business and your real estate portfolio, they nevertheless play a significant role in your Impenetrable Financial Legacy.

By being relentless in hitting "your number", you will have achieved a level of investment in this asset class to not only fund your retirement, but to leave a legacy. With admirable yet readily achievable targets, your index funds will provide for your retirement without drawing down on them. That's right, you can live off the income, not disrupting the base asset.

Having set your number to this level means that you do not need to draw down on your business or your real estate. Every asset class can continue with the same momentum – talk about a legacy!

Cash and Liquidity

Protecting your legacy from short-term challenges – e.g., times of negative cash flow in your business, an unexpected renovation within your real estate portfolio – requires having liquidity that does not require you to decrease your investment base across any of your three asset classes.

I have seen many entrepreneurs, including myself, give up long-term assets, reducing their wealth-accumulating base, to solve a short-term cash problem. Don't do that. Keep adequate liquidity.

Liquidity not only reduces risk, but further allows you to take advantage of opportunities as they arise – e.g., purchasing power during a stock market crash or giving you the ability to execute on a business acquisition.

Putting It All Together

Imagine your best future self. Where are you? What are you doing? Who are you doing it with? Inevitably, you will be surrounded by people that you love and admire, and that love and admire you. You will be in great health, without restrictions, to enjoy your best future self.

But none of this is possible without being intentional towards all three pillars of life – relationships, health and financial freedom. As every aspect of your life affects the others.

In this book, we have tackled the foundation – financial independence.

Imagine a world where you have achieved this Impenetrable Financial Legacy.

Everything in this book is achievable. Employed together in sequence, a disciplined execution of these tactics places you well into the top 1% of net worth holders across the country. And that is just the start of it. That is the base that will continue to grow exponentially into retirement and propel future generations into meaningful prosperity. Your kids' kids' kids will have a running head start on life.

You have wealth. You have choice. You have freedom.

With your business as the economic engine of your personal financial legacy, you have a unique opportunity to get this right – an opportunity not afforded to the general population, not offered to the nine-to-fivers.

Having the will to execute the three asset classes in the way presented here, you have the opportunity to build significant wealth. Wealth that fosters a mindset beyond yourself, but of creating a legacy for future generations. A mindset that they will inherit, an asset base that they will inherit. Putting those two together is a dynamite combination that provides the best assurance for exponential growth beyond your time on earth.

Look at yourself as a custodian for future generations, whereby your wealth building isn't subject to stages and life transitions of retirement and death; rather, your decisions have an inter-generational outlook. By doing so, your wealth is not subject to the starts and stops, the wind downs and dispositions. Rather, it continues to accumulate in perpetuity.

For more information or to connect with the author, visit www.gregbott.com.

For Product Safety Concerns and Information please contact our EU representative GPSR@taylorandfrancis.com
Taylor & Francis Verlag GmbH, Kaufingerstraße 24, 80331 München, Germany

www.ingramcontent.com/pod-product-compliance
Ingram Content Group UK Ltd.
Pitfield, Milton Keynes, MK11 3LW, UK
UKHW022344190926
475702UK00015B/2088
9781041168386